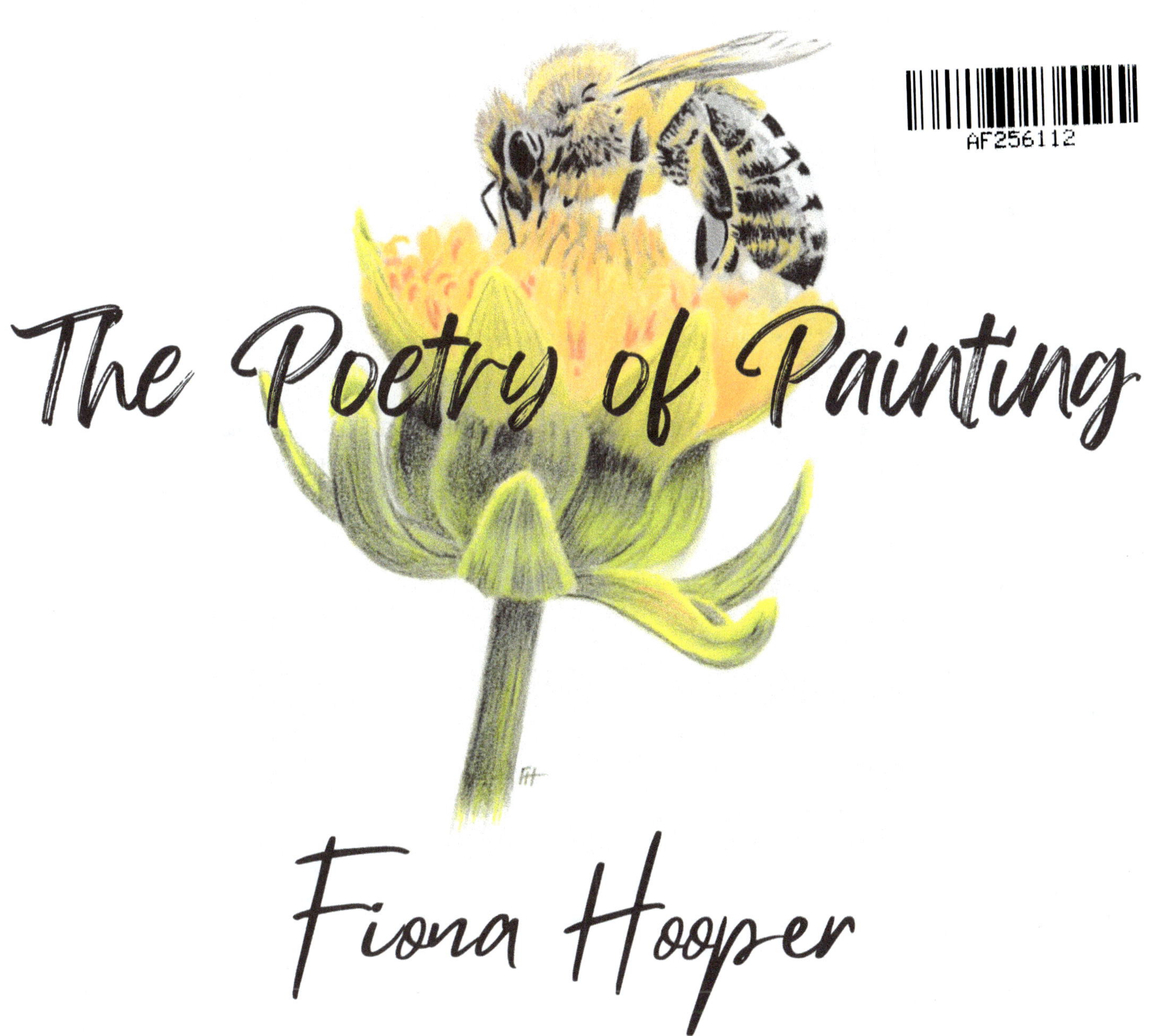

# The Poetry of Painting

## Fiona Hooper

Cover image: © Fiona Hooper - FionaHooper.com

Cover design: Ritesh Nigam - ritesh.uk



Published in 2022 by Fiona Hooper in association with Inkdness, United Kingdom
Book Publishing Mentor: Ritesh Nigam - ritesh.uk



**A personal thank you to my supporters shown below who went the extra mile in helping to make this book a reality:**

**Barbara A. Heath**
**Simon Hill**
**Barbara Anna Martin FRSA**
**Linda Parry-Smith**
**Dave Webb**

First Printing, 2022
ISBN - 978-1-915857-01-9 (Paperback)
ISBN - 978-1-915857-02-6 (eBook)
ISBN - 978-1-915857-03-3 (Hardback)

# Dedication

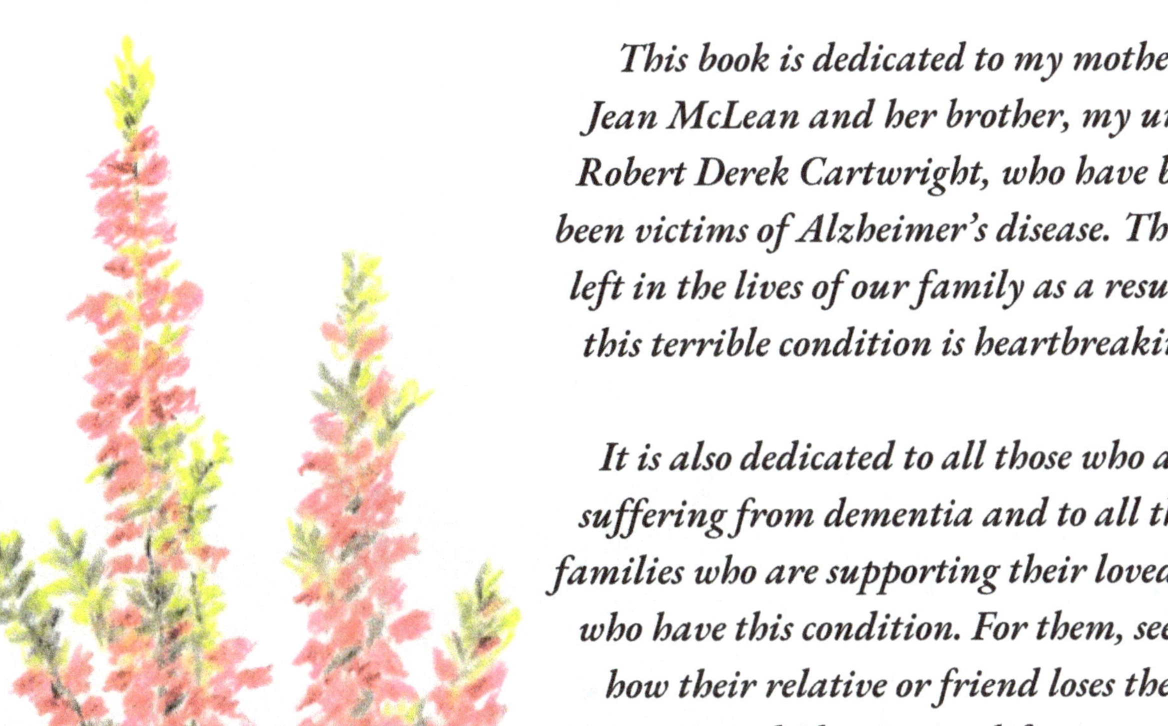

*This book is dedicated to my mother Jean McLean and her brother, my uncle Robert Derek Cartwright, who have both been victims of Alzheimer's disease. The gap left in the lives of our family as a result of this terrible condition is heartbreaking.*

*It is also dedicated to all those who are suffering from dementia and to all those families who are supporting their loved ones who have this condition. For them, seeing how their relative or friend loses their memories and identity is a life sentence and arguably harder to cope with than those suffering the disease directly.*

*I hope that this book will help to one day put an end to this dreadful disease.*

**In aid of Alzheimer's Research UK**

# Foreword 

Art has been vital in my life and brought me so much joy and peace. Looking at the wonderful paintings and poems in Fiona's book, I am reminded of the connection that art can bring between people and importantly our memories of place, friends and family. I have seen how art can open those doors that seem shut for good in the people we love the most. This is a glorious book both for the eyes and the heart.

It is also doing something else truly remarkable.... If you are reading this and bought Fiona's beautiful book, then I must say thank you. You along with Fiona have contributed to vital dementia research that will support Alzheimer's Research UK's battle mission to overcome the condition that took both my parents and affects millions in this country and around the world. We have seen the power of what scientific research can do fighting a pandemic, and we must now use that example and find a cure for dementia.

Thanks to people like Fiona who have seen the effects of dementia first-hand, we can and must raise enough money to make a cure a reality.

**Anneka Rice**
Artist, broadcaster and Alzheimer's Research UK supporter

# Acknowledgments

I had never imagined how much effort would be needed nor how much reward would be gained from writing and publishing this second book of my art.  However, I would never have gotten this far without the generous contributions of time, content, advice, guidance and support given to me by a whole range of people.  This is my opportunity to say a heartfelt thank you to all who have been involved with this project.

This book is a collection of my paintings and accompanying poems written by 10 amazing internationally known poets using my paintings as inspiration.  I am hugely indebted to all these wonderful poets for sharing their beautiful poems on my weekly live shows and for allowing me to reproduce their poems in this book.  Their talent and generosity know no bounds.  Thank you - Martin Goldie, Rosie Hodson, Bernard Jacobs, Oscar Nicholson, Ritesh Nigam, Roz Ottery, Aliberry SP,  Markey Mark Symmonds, Yvonne Ugarte and Skylar J Wynter.

I would like to offer a special thank you to Anneka Rice for taking time out of her busy schedule to write this forward for my book and for being so supportive of this project.  I am humbled and immensely grateful.

I also owe a huge debt of gratitude to Ritesh Nigam who, besides being a talented poet, has guided me through the process of publishing this book and the crowdfunding required to get to this point.  Ritesh has been a model of patience, creativity and support.  His good humour and knowledge have kept me going when it seemed that there was far too much to realistically achieve in the time available.

I must also thank all my friends and colleagues who are too many to mention individually by name but who have provided support and encouragement to me to bring this book to publication, especially given that it is being sold to raise funds for Alzheimer's Research.  My thanks to you all.

Finally, I must thank my family and in particular my partner Chris for his support and encouragement with this undertaking, for providing me with endless cups of tea and glasses of wine to keep the creative juices flowing, and for being a listening ear both when things were 'difficult' and when celebrations were in order.

To you all, my deepest and most heartfelt thanks, love and appreciation.

**Fiona Hooper**
**October 2022**

# Contents 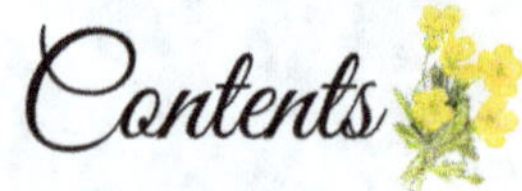

#  Introduction

The book that nearly never was!

During the pandemic lockdown of 2020, I signed up for an online art marketing course as other more traditional ways of promoting my art had come to a temporary halt.

One of the challenges of the course was to 'go live' on social media – presenting myself and my art live in front of the camera – not something that I had ever done before and also not something that sat comfortably with me. But I got stuck in and found that it really wasn't as bad as I had thought and tried not to be too critical of myself.

Later in the course another challenge was presented – to do a live show each week with a set theme running throughout - and I decided on 'The Poetry Of Painting' as my theme. I began by delving into all the different forms of poetry, including the discovery that there is actually a word for poetry written about art - ekphrastic!

I sought out poetry that had been written about art and artists, moved on to songs in rhyming verse about paintings and painters, and then had the idea of writing a poem or two myself to go with my paintings. This was followed by my brainwave to invite poets to join me on the shows and to read a poem that they had written about one of my paintings, followed by me reading my poem about the same work.

I was thrilled to find that poets were very keen to join in with this project, and each wrote their poem(s) without us first discussing the chosen painting in any way, meaning that it was purely their direct response to the art that formed the basis of their poems.

I believe art is about memory.

Whether it's visualising a place you've been, imagining a place that doesn't exist, or even understanding your connection to a place, it will all rest on your memories. Your memories of who you are, what you've done, where you've been, and most importantly with whom those memories were created.

Since childhood, my mother loved taking me to places with wonderful natural scenery, which has subsequently inspired my landscape paintings. As someone whose mother is in a care home due to Alzheimer's, I've witnessed the pain of losing those memories and losing that connection.

That's why I'm publishing this poetry book inspired by art in aid of Alzheimer's Research UK. After successfully crowdfunding £2025 with 57 supporters within 14 days, I am thrilled to present this one-of-a-kind collection of poetry and my paintings.

So, sit back, relax and indulge in the calming, tranquil landscapes surrounded by evocative words.

# Poet Bios

## Fiona Hooper

Fiona's passion lies in painting landscapes in her distinctive and contemporary style. She works predominantly in oils using a painting knife, to capture the peace and tranquillity of the wild, natural places that she loves to discover.

Exploring and visiting these places is an excellent way of recharging her mental 'batteries'. Directly connected to these visits, Fiona creates paintings that transport people to a place of calm helping them to relax, unwind and find inner peace. She also often incorporates gold and silver leaf in her paintings.

Wherever possible Fiona likes to work directly from the subject, painting in the open air in the places that she loves, interpreting the sights, sounds and smells in paint on canvas. But, when this is not possible, her sketches, photographs, and memories act as the inspiration for her paintings.

Her work has won both awards and critical acclaim and can be found in collections in the UK and internationally, including the USA, Canada, France, Ireland, Malta, Australia, and Switzerland.

Fiona lives & works in West Sussex, UK, where she is often to be found on location with her easel and paints.

She occasionally accepts commissions for landscape paintings, creating lasting and treasured memories of special places beautifully interpreted in her unique style, and is an accomplished professional portrait artist having completed many successful commissions of both people and animals.

https://linktr.ee/fionahooper

## Aliberry SP

Ali SP was born and raised on the beautiful island of St. Lucia. She currently resides in Georgia, where she longs to hear the waves and smell and taste the saltiness of the ocean.

She is a health care professional and an artist who enjoys writing short stories and poetry. When she is not writing and painting, she spends time with friends and loved ones and is a great aunt to her brother's two dogs, Klaus and Arya.

She received an editor's choice award for her poem 'Black Girl Magic', published in the Paterson Literary Review, issue #50 (Spring 2022). She was also awarded an honourable mention for her poem 'Painting Me' from the Writer's Digest.

https://medium.com/@alist12

## Bernard Jacobs

Bernard has always enjoyed writing but had done little until he joined a SCOLA Creative Writing class with Stephen Smith. Stephen is a great teacher and encouraged Bernard to write short stories and, increasingly, poetry.

Bernard joined Sutton Writers, became Chair, and is currently Treasurer and leads the Sutton Writers Poetry Workshop. He has won prizes for his poetry, and has written and self-published three books, The Nonsuch Poems, 168 Miles Between Stanzas, and In Light and Shade. Bernard judges competitions, edits and produces books and pamphlets, and runs workshops for adults and in schools.

In his business life he owned his own company, advising companies on business continuity - how to avoid and recover from disasters.

Bernard has a wonderful family; a wife and three children, all married, and nine grandchildren. For relaxation he reads, sings in a church choir, loves sport, and of course writes.

For more information about his writing please go to The Beeches Writer at www.bernardjacobs.com

## Markey Mark Symmonds

Markey Mark Symmonds is a poetry and flash fiction writer and performer. He started writing poetry as a teenager, returning to it after meeting his wife in 1992. He made up and recited poetry while they sat by a local lake.

Markey Mark didn't write poetry again until he was 46 after being diagnosed with dyslexia and dysgraphia, and then retook his GCSE English language qualification passing at Level B. This proved to be a new lease of life for him.

In 2017 he started writing poetry at a phenomenal rate on his blog to share his words with the world. He published numerous poems online and started performing his poetry at a local open mic night, enabling him to watch and listen to poets perform, and started attending many open mic events.

Markey Mark has had work published in online journals and printed anthologies both in the UK and internationally.

During the pandemic of 2020, Markey Mark performed around the world on Zoom, including Nashville, Perth and Melbourne (Australia), and Scotland. Markey Mark has published his first collection 'Rhythm of the Ink - The First Wave', and his work has featured on local radio.

https://linktr.ee/Rhythmoftheink

# Rosie Hodson

Rosie is a house portrait artist from Hertfordshire in the UK. She always loved art, poetry and music at school and frequently wrote poems and, later, songs for the purposes of entertainment.

Although she did not study music Rosie always had an ear for melodies and harmonies which she put to good use as a primary teacher, and then an early years music and movement business owner!

This work came to an abrupt end with Covid 19. Rosie now paints watercolour portraits of people's homes and special places. Over the last 2 years her work has continued to develop, combining her father's skills in architectural drawing with her mother's love of vibrant colour to produce highly detailed, colourful house, church and pub portraits. She specialises in painting sunshine and shadow, and reflections in windows or water.

Rosie also writes songs about many of the buildings she paints especially those that have interesting stories or legends attached to them. She has thoroughly enjoyed appearing on Fiona's live show to share her songs about Fiona's amazing work! Strangely only one of the three paintings she chose featured buildings!

https://rosiehodsononlyonelikeit.co.uk/

# Roz Ottery

Roz Ottery started Britain's first SINGING TELEGRAM business in1979 and won the Daily Telegraph and Heineken 'New Business Of The Year' in 1981.

As a performer she enjoyed 5 years of success on the professional stage, such as playing 'Magenta' in Rocky Horror. For further development, Roz trained as a clown. In this capacity she was honoured and privileged to represent Britain internationally in Japan. Roz eventually retrained, as a psychotherapist, for the NHS, until she retired.

Roz has been writing poetry since she was 7 years old. The poems were her secret love until 2018 when she made a brave decision to share her work and joined the internet group 'NORTHERN POETRY'. Roz has achieved first place in 4 of their competitions. Next venture was 'FOUR WOMEN POETS FOR THE ENVIRONMENT' in 2018/2019 in the North of England.

Roz has been published in two anthologies. The 2019 'THE HIGH WOLDS' - this collection is an arts council publication - and the 2021 anthology of horror 'FROM THE SHADOWS' edited by Amanda Steel. Roz is still shy about her poetry. It remains very close to her heart. She feels progress is 'one step at a time' but is determined to continue.

## Skylar J Wynter

Skylar J Wynter is the best-selling author of poetry and flash fiction collection 'Pieces of Humanity' released on October 10th 2020 to align with National Mental Health month.

After an incident which changed the course of her life in 2014, Wynter turned to various art forms to process the trauma and make sense of her new self. She shares her poetry in the hopes it will help others find peace within their own realities and encourage humanity to reach out to each other with decency.

Skylar resides in the Perth Hills of Western Australia, where she pens her creations overlooking national parkland. When she is not writing she likes to create beautiful things with her limited jewellery making and sculpting skills, and serene spaces in her garden. She loves a great book, a sunny day and witnessing humans behaving decently. She hates cooking, and injustice, hopes Covid-19 disappears and online poetry events don't, and that someone finds a way to make celery taste like cheesecake.

https://linktr.ee/Skylarjwynter

## Oscar Nicholson

Oscar Nicholson is currently in his final year of a degree in English Literature from Durham University (2022). He has always been interested in poetry but never thought he was capable of writing it.

Oscar started writing 'poems' – scribbles in the notes section of his phone – during the winter lockdown of late 2020-2021 and when he showed them to friends the reaction wasn't the 'this is awful' he was expecting but instead 'this is bearable'. He has now developed a real love for writing poetry and connecting through it.

Oscar met Fiona exhibiting her art in Kingston where he was intrigued by the painting 'Venice Dreams' and decided to write some rough lines. A month later he was on her show with a full poem based on the same painting and has now been on more of her shows.

Oscar feels that poetry and painting are mutually enforcing art forms and thinks the combination of visual and verbal creation produces utterly organic, different and beautiful expressions from all minds. He encourages anyone – whether it be for painting, poetry or any other form of expression – to pick up the relevant tool (pen, brush, phone etc.) and create as it's so therapeutic!

## Martin Goldie

Martin Goldie was born in 1959 and lives and works in Argyll, Scotland, with his wife Janice and their dogs. In his spare time he is a keen hillwalker, and he also loves reading and listening to music.

He started writing poetry in 2020 and many of his poems are inspired by the beautiful mountains and glens of Scotland where he loves to walk, and the stories and history of the areas he visits.

Martin enjoys reading his poetry to live audiences at the various open-mic sessions in and around Glasgow and also at online poetry events.

His poetry has already won multiple awards and has been published in numerous magazines and anthologies both in the UK and internationally.

2022 sees him working on a new collection of poems for publication.

## Yvonne Ugarte

Yvonne has been writing for as long as she can remember, writing her first poem at the tender age of five. She is a published author, song writer and ventriloquist!

Yvonne's second book – "My Aunt Jean's A Dinosaur" - consists of poetry that she has written for children over the last 50 years and is beautifully illustrated by the children at Beeston Primary School where she works. All monies raised are for the Martin House Children's Hospice who cared so lovingly for her little boy. Yvonne has already presented them with £900 from the sales of this book and is proud to announce that Waterstones is going to stock it - an achievement of which she is rightly very proud.

Yvonne's book can be obtained via her publisher at www.runciblespoonpress.co.uk, only £10 plus p&p.

# Ritesh Nigam

Ritesh Nigam is an Indian-origin poet living in the leafy suburbs of Earley in Berkshire, England.

While struggling with mental health illness and suicidal thoughts in 2017, he found a ray of inspiration in the form of Ernest Hemingway's six-word story and penned down 50 thought-provoking stories in one night. He went on to publish a collection of thought-provoking six-word stories through crowdfunding and got featured in the local press.

During the pandemic, he turned to writing poetry and created his own poetic style called Link Poetry, a spin-off of loop poetry and now expresses himself exclusively in Link poetry style.

When he is not running or cycling long distances or taking picturesque photos, he can be found mentoring others to write, publish & market their books through his charity-driven publishing platform called Inkdness (an anagram of kindness).

His works can be found on ritesh.uk

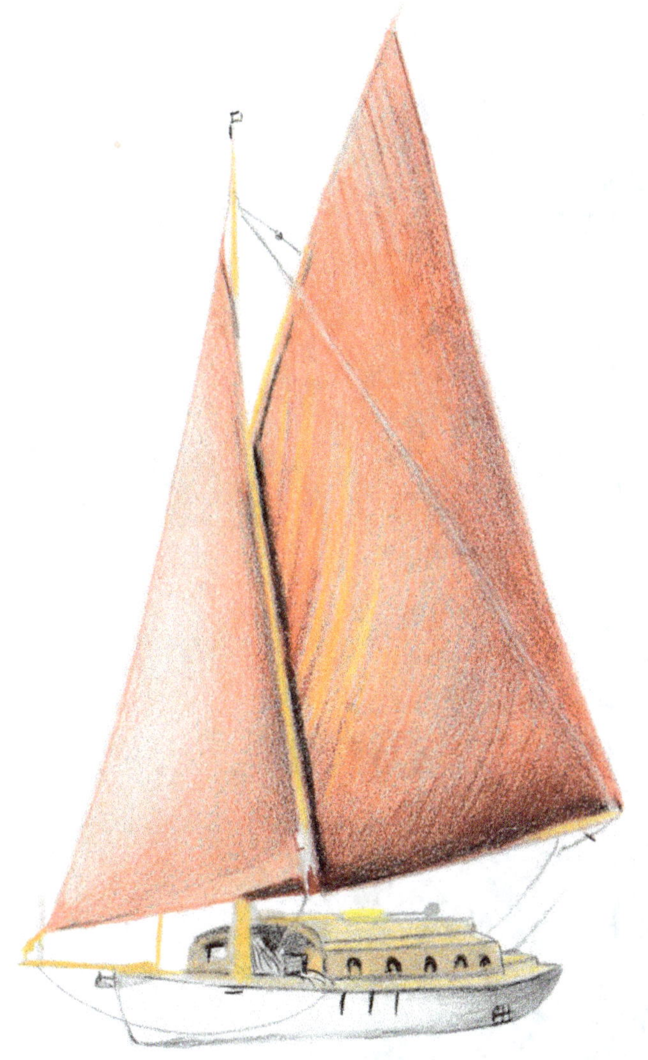

# Softly Through The Canyon

Oil on canvas, 60 x 30 cms.

# Softly Through The Canyon

Softly through the canyon,
Moving with grace and care,
Stepping over fallen branches,
Enjoying the cool moist air.

Relish the gentle murmurings
As the cycle of life abounds,
Sensing rather than hearing
The barely audible sounds.

The soft scents of damp leaves,
The caress of a branch hanging down,
Listening, looking, feeling,
Now doesn't that beat a dirty old town???

**Fiona Hooper** © 2021

The wind creeps softly through the canyon
oxygenating trees as they sway in the breeze
ignited in the fire of golden leaves.
Autumnal death upon the wind's gentle breath.

To dappled sky, the foliage reaches as though
desperate to escape this canyon before one by one
on the winds their leaves fly until the bareness
of their trunks silhouetted against the autumn sky.

With every day every hour every minute,
the blueness of the sky shows itself moving softly
through that glacial carving.
Adding to the picturesque wealth,
framing the fire by cunning stealth.

Then the wind stops and the canyon is silent
the wilderness of sound, just leaves of fire whispering
as they expire and dance their ritual to the ground
where they bond with earth helping spring's rebirth.

**Markey Mark Symmonds** © 2022

# Summer Pastures

Oil on canvas, 30 x 60 cms.

# Summer Pastures

An afternoon stroll on a dreamy summer's day,
Dragonflies darting here and there,
A dog barks in the distance,
The sound carried by the still, languid air.

I hear the gentle hum of bees collecting nectar,
Searching for flowers in the warm grass,
Reflections of the clear blue sky and distant barn,
In a surface as smooth as glass.

Small insects skate lazily across the water,
So inviting for cooling hot toes,
Sitting quietly, watching the hole in the bank,
Was that a water vole's furry brown nose?

The lull of activity in the heat of the day,
The warmth of the sun on our backs,
Linger a while on the old wooden bridge,
It's way too soon to be making tracks.

Pull a stem of grass and chew on the end,
Let your mind wander and be free,
Take time to be in tune with nature,
It'll be good for you, try it and see.

**Fiona Hooper** © 2021

The scent of hot grass and Oaktree leaves on morning breeze
Serenades Summer.
The haze over distant trees tells me air is thick with humidity
Even before I step outside and breathe
Inhaling warm air drenched in honeysuckle joy and the hum of
bees.

Foamy clouds whitewash blue skies and my heart knows
SAD, for a moment, is gone
carried away by the steady beat of dragonfly wings
And birdsong
Lazy water slides by with barely a murmur
suspending fat trout between smooth rock bottom
and glassy surface and I wonder,
How is it emotions are so easily manipulated,
spiralling inwards
And outwards
with the changing of seasons?
Is our sense of well-being forever tied to
The ancient rhythms of cyclical survival
Is this warm glow of content a shadow remnant,
of primitive cultures rejoicing in transient abundance?
What is it about sunshine, warmth and earthy smells
That saturates our cells
with hope?
I don't know,
But
I rejoice in the euphony of Azure skies, and cricket song
Of warm breeze and sunlight filtered
through spreadeagled fingers
Of daylight hours extended into
Balmy twilight and silent darkness
Descending over summer pastures.

**Skylar J Wynter** © 2022

# Shepherd's Sunrise

Oil on canvas, 30 x 60 cms.

# Shepherd's Sunrisee

A gentle light,
Clouds lit from below,
Sunlight reflecting on the waves,
Surf, changed from white to gold,
Waves rolling in, creating mirrors,
The sand shifting in colour,
Brown, blue, ochre.

Walk barefoot,
The feel of sand on skin,
The cool water between toes,
The rush of foam around ankles,
Cool, invigorating, refreshing,
It's worth the early alarm,
To have this moment.

Another day,
A blank page waiting,
Full of possibility and promise,
Gulls call, soaring on the breeze,
The sea mist clearing in the sun,
The day banishing the night,
Excitement in the air.

Breath, inhale,
The fresh ocean air,
Feel alive in this open space,
Be part of nature and feed your soul,
Let the sea breeze clear your mind,
Return invigorated, energised,
Make this your day!

**Fiona Hooper © 2021**

# Shepherd's Sunrise

"The Shepherd's Sunrise" speaks.
It whispers wonders of the world, whose beauty can not be confined.
NOT a product of imaginings.
But a legacy of 'being'. A teaching for the emotionally blind.

For each wonder of this world can 'speak' to our immortal soul.
Like lambs calling to the Shepherd to find home; part of the 'Whole'.
Beneath thought, deep within our essence, is a connection for us all.
A moment when hearts bond; cry out in joy; in peace; in love; in awe.

This broken world has little space for 'wonders'
and time we squander.
So we fight for our existence and clamour to find meaning,
too fast to pause, too important to ponder.

We seek to repair ourselves, only through 'doing' which binds our life to gain...
and a painting like this, echoes the eternal ribbon of life:
Releases our vision and breaks that bond and chain.

Artists connect to 'the whole', to heal the wounds of dissonant harmful feeling.
They make time for 'wonder' and are drawn to capture it, treasure it,
share its worth and healing.

Behold! There! A night ending; resplendent by displays of celestial majesty.
The firmament.
Mankind's leveller.
Enticing us to look into the eternal tapestry.

Yesterday's failures cease...
within a night's silent reverie
Out of that darkness, an emerging dawn seeps light,
heralded by unspeakable beauty.

So humbling in its simple resplendence.
Casting an ocean of possibility across our vision.
It warms our hope, repairs a broken spirit.
in pinks and blues; creams and orange.
to walk on... in renewed precision.

So, when you seek hope, think of
'A Shepherd's sunrise'.
And look to the ocean
for constancy.
Look to the dawn's colours
for clarity.
Look to the burgeoning light
for inner calm.

This dawn, lovingly composed, here,
is confirmation of our connectivity...
and it is this, the artist holds, within their palm.

**Roz Ottery** ©2022

# *Beautiful Birches*

**Oil on canvas, 16 x 16 ins.**

Majestic they stand, in the quiet woods,
Patiently waiting for the season to turn,
Growing, forming buds for new leaves,
Towering above the tight coils of the fern.

Individual and unique,
They stand as though asleep,
Bare branches waiting in silhouette,
Looking down where the brambles creep.

So distinctive the bark on their trunks,
A patchwork of white, black and grey,
Like ebony and ivory, staccato patterns,
Or a giant's paintbrush has been at play.

The smell of the damp leaf litter,
Last year's leaves crisp under boot,
There's new life in the rich soil,
Ideal for fungi to grow and to fruit.

Their leaves will be delicate,
Unfurling way up on high,
Clean, fresh and green,
Creating fractals against the sky.

But for now they wait,
As the days grow longer,
The sap is rising,
And the buds grow stronger.

The brambles will spring into life,
The coils of the ferns extend,
Branches with new leafy mantles,
Towards the earth will bend.

**Fiona Hooper** © 2021

My trunks stand strong, dressed in this silver lining
That holds the core of my still beating soul deep within side,
Branches devoid of leaves that have long since left to hide,
Leaving me barren of colour in the autumn of my days
That evaporate amongst the sun's low haze,
As it bounces the fauna around shedding brightness and light
All around from the foliage that changes with time.

The bareness of the branches preventing what little life I have
Still coursing through my veins being sucked dry
By the immense heat that keeps the flora glistening at my feet.
You miss the beauty of the surrounding palette
As you salivate over my armoured core.

But with passing time my body slowly renourishes itself,
Bit by bit, leaf by leaf, growing until the spectacular sight
That is the great birch has blossomed once more,
Allowed to reach my full glory in the heat of the midday sun,
Until the season changes again and my outer beauty is shed
Leaving that silvered protective core
Cutting through the landscape once more.

**Markey Mark Symmonds** © 2021

# Solacee Of The Trees

**Oil on canvas, 50 x 50 cms**

Rich glowing colours,
Gold and orange hues,
Soft greens down below,
Peacefulness ensues.

The shady forest floor,
Trunks rising high,
Reaching for the light,
Reaching for the sky.

Birdsong in the canopy,
Deer move like ghosts,
The forest in motion,
With the life that it hosts.

Nurture your soul,
Let go of tension,
Immerse yourself here,
In nature's invention.

Escape from the rat race,
Put aside care,
Enjoy the tranquillity,
Just enjoy being there.

So when life is tough,
And you're down on your knees,
Head for the forest,
And the solace of the trees.

**Fiona Hooper** © 2021

This vista greets my soul in stunning flame –

To merge and then to swell; and call my name!

Long boughs, like thought, rise up toward the dappled light.

And titian branch of orange flare, fills me with rare delight.

The hues and shades entwine above, like love's 'first kiss' released…

as the mantle of the trees gives me belonging: Gives me peace.

**Roz Ottery** © 2021

Hooper

# *Whispering Waters*

**Oil on canvas, 50 x 50 cms.**

It winds, with curves like a fulsome body,
Meandering lazily, slowly, gently,
Arcs created by the power of water,
By sheep and wild ponies who visit to drink.

A sheltered valley nestling between high moors,
The cool moist air nurturing the lichen and moss,
Drifting autumn mists, softening the trees,
Muting and absorbing sound in this quiet place.

Gentle currents carry leaves on glassy surface,
Dark depths of rich colour and translucent water,
Serene and placid after dry days and nights,
The russet shore of leaves lying undisturbed.

But come the storm unleashed upon the hills,
The pool once calm, now stygian, turbulent,
Covered in foam, the torrent in full flow,
Carving its channel through the valley floor.

But this will pass, the spate will subside,
The freshly washed valley, colours glowing bright,
Once more the peacefulness and calm return,
And silence apart from the whispering waters.

**F**iona **H**ooper © 2021

Meandering through the golden yellows and fire burned oranges, slowly creeping along your channels, spreading to fill all the cracks day after day I roll along gently permeating your barriers. Eroding your seams until the shell gives way slowly slipping and sliding into the glow of my life crumbling where the abrasions cut like a knife. The slow coercion of bubbling streams filled with the wreckage of your nature dreams.

The colours of your palette diminished to brown as the silt and loam start to give ground. You try to contain me to divert and drown. The weir pushes me over the edge where the cast out dead wreckage of hollowed out trees linger as the white tips of my fluidity soak your earth deeper down.

The constant flow through green pastures yet untouched by browning earth that waits for the amebous of existence to start their resistance. Trickling weaving power of the stream that breathes life with toxic vibes into green and pleasant lands. As it's toxicity slowly expanding as it cuts, your lifeline leaving scars on its shoreline.

**Markey Mark Symmonds** © 2021

# Still Waters Run Deep

Oil on canvas, 40 x 60 cms

# Still Waters Run Deep

**Oil on canvas, 40 x 60 cms.**

It rises high in the lofty mountains,
Barely a trickle in its many tributaries,
Joining forces as they follow gravity's pull,
Like the landscape's meshed capillaries.

This myriad of diminutive streams,
Meeting, merging, growing in strength,
Tumbling freely down rough, steep slopes,
Starting the journey of the river's length.

Slowing, calming, as the gradient eases,
Clear, cold water, gliding deep and dark,
Nurturing the abundant life around it,
Sculpting its banks, leaving its mark.

Where wild beasts roam, and eagles soar,
From steep mountain to wide open space,
Always moving inexorably down its valley,
Flowing with inevitability and grace.

Drifting lazily now with silent mystery,
Its surface smooth, glassy, as it feigns sleep,
Currents melding in its hidden depths,
The power is there - still waters run deep.

**Fiona Hooper** © 2021

After a rough, rocky journey, here it rests,

Rests upon this serene tranquil scenery

Scenery manned by short green trees

Trees whose shortness seems deliberate

Deliberate to remain close enough to listen to it.

It, the youthful water that made the journey. If,

If the waters could speak out boldly

Boldly it would tell of its adventures and troubles

Troubles only known and acknowledged by the old lake

Lake that lies beneath the snowy Alps, silently and still

Still it holds secrets of that adventurous journey

Journey now almost forgotten and buried deep

Deep and lightyears away from still calm surface.

**Ritesh Nigam** © 2021

Hooper

# Ruffled Waters

**Oil on canvas, 40 x 40 cms**


High in the distant foothills,
Where the air is crystal clear,
Fed by the mountain springs,
This remote and peaceful mere.

Nestled below the craggy peaks,
Reflecting their misty violet hue,
The snow-capped rocky sentinels,
Sharp against the vibrant blue.

A zephyr gently stirs the reeds,
And whispers softly in the trees,
Caressing the pines and the bushes,
Reflections broken by the breeze.

Ripples like miniature breakers,
Tipped with delicate foamy white,
Breaking quietly on the shore,
Sparkling in the crystalline light.

These ruffled waters clean and clear,
Summer refuge for bird and beast,
The balmy warmth now tempered,
By the tendrils of winter from the East.


**Fiona Hooper** © 2021

Out beyond the water's edge,
the glassy surface, yesterday impervious
to even a ripple, begins to ruffle.
A reflection of all that's
unsettled beneath my skin.
Things I contain. Keep in.
Anchoring them offshore
to prevent onshore pandemonium.
Exhaling, the zephyr of my breath
joins with wind until I breathe in.
Stealing back what I gave
just as the waves
draw back into natures container,
the grit that will form another layer,
of a foundation impervious
to the activity on the surface.
The waves lapping at the waters-edge,
are nothing that the shoreline can not manage.
The breeze triggering the rippling,
is not decimating but, cleansing.
The colours of reeds and mosses muted,
are daily transmuted,
with changing skies.
This is where truth lies, I realise.
Here. There. Somewhere in between the glare,
of full sun on a summer's day
and a landscape filtered grey,
when dark clouds ballet
over mountain tops.
A landscape never lies. It may change.
May appear unfamiliar. Different.
But its truth on any given day
is reflective only of the light that shines on it.


**Skylar J Wynter** © 2021

# Dartmoor Cottages

Oil on canvas, 40 x 50 cms.

# Dartmoor Cottages

**Oil on canvas, 40 x 50 cms**

Nestling in a sheltered valley,
Between a rough track and a stream,
Solid, with thick walls of local granite,
The cottages watch and wait.

Impervious to the soft rain that falls,
And insulating against summer's heat,
A safe and welcoming refuge,
Whatever the mood of the land.

These walls have borne witness,
They've seen birth and death,
Comforting in their endurance,
A home and retreat for so many.

Out of the gate and onto the moors,
Follow the track to Wistman's Wood,
The 'clatter' of granite boulders,
Providing shelter for twisted roots.

Ancient, gnarled oaks, dwarf in stature,
Their contorted forms festooned,
Limbs covered with hanging, living drapery,
Swathes of primeval lichen and moss.

As the sun descends on its arc,
The valley is shrouded in shadow,
Time to return once again,
To the haven of a Dartmoor cottage.

**Fiona Hooper** © 2021

**(Song)**

I've walked this well worn country lane more times than I can say

With its fringe of bushy grasses hiding rocks of stony grey

And the shrouded misty hills ahead mask the sun's last feeble ray

As I come home

And the creamy walls of welcome call from beneath their crowns of slate

And I know that he'll be worried cos I said I'd not be late

But the fire will be burning brightly in the old cast iron grate

And I am home

The silky silver puddles fill the dimples on the ground

In the stillness of the misty air, the birds the only sound

And the barren trees of winter dig their roots deep in the ground

And I am home

And the creamy walls of welcome call from beneath their crowns of slate

And I know that he'll be worried cos I said I'd not be late

But the fire will be burning brightly in the old cast iron grate

And I am home

**Rosie Hodson** © 2021

A Hooper

# *Blustery Day*

**Oil on canvas, 30 x 30 cms**

A leaf, dry and light as a feather, carried by an unseen hand,
Tossing and turning, bowling along, then dropped,
Only to be lifted again to resume its fitful journey.

Fresh green shoots of crops clothe the land like velvet,
The surface disturbed by the wind's turbulent caress,
A multitude of supple young stalks bending to its will.

The breeze moves on, takes hold of the still bare trees,
As if vexed by the solid trunks it rattles the leafless twigs,
Their brittle sound adding to the wind's own voice.

While shadows of scudding clouds skate over the land below,
Flurries of invisible gusts tug at hair and clothes,
With the insistence of a small child that's being ignored.

It's the type of weather that blows away the cobwebs,
Brings colour to pale cheeks and fresh ideas to mind,
And having blown moves on, taking with it this blustery day.

**Fiona Hooper** © 2021

The wind whispers old wisdom through the silence of this place.
My secluded boughs have always reached; stretched forlornly into space.
Watching guardians point upwards... and so it is with jaded eye
I see the gales make blue grey clouds play out sad battles in the sky.

Each thought I'd shaped around the bare branched 'trio of the moor'.
This my only destination but I've not felt these thoughts before.
All the bluster of the blast, helps blow the cobwebs far and free
Are Macbeth's weird sisters laughing? I am one... they are 'The Three'.

I'm that captivated presence, standing bare, my wood like stone...
There are none to bear me witness. I've faced all scrutiny alone.
But these winds of change swirl round me with a flash of pure insight...
The Three's branches reach towards me... Or... is that just a trick of light?

Could it be my "isolation" was a self-inflicted fate?
And the ivy threaded o'er me, protects what I'd advocate?
Are those others in the distance... surrounds of misty, hazy hedge,
Only trying to defend me from those gusts, at storm's rough edge?

All these years I've felt alone here as the rain has come and gone.
Wondered, as the leaves were falling... if I wanted to go on?
Now I see The Three, quite differently; gifts of nature's far foresight...
Too many years I've languished... blind to peril of my plight.

I'm the green-grey imperfection, with a dab and smudge of black,
Standing under stunning skies that border fields along the track.
This stiff breeze gave whispered counsel... as it danced and brushed and curled:
Calling "Your place is within this picture, adding focus for the world".


**Roz Ottery** © 2021

## Moored Up

Oil on board, 10 x 12 ins

# Moored Up

**Oil on board, 10 x 12 ins.**

By the old boat shed, resting quietly now,
The silent boat waits, moored stern and bow.
With hull of pale blue, and mast standing proud,
Its tarpaulin covering, by way of a shroud.

The boat bides its time, sails neatly furled,
Protected by fenders, inured to the world.
What tales it could tell, of outings in the sun,
Racing other yachts, and paddle boats outrun.

It's had some adventures, it hopes it still will,
During the summer, before autumn's chill.
Stopping for picnics, without running aground,
Watching the wildlife, without making a sound.

In these quiet waters, sheltered and still,
It longs to be moving, it yearns for a thrill.
Its day will come, its people return,
Then off they will sail, with dad in the stern.

**Fiona Hooper** © 2021

Reflections dapple the placid broad;

tranquil and serene

a small, blue boat nestles against the bank,

sails furled, decks tarpaulin covered.

The bare mast, wired with a taut strumming stay,

bisects the length of the red-roofed barn behind

and lances into the trees beyond.

Dark fenders guard and protect.

The primary colours lead me to the vanishing point

of the treeline. Another day I might pass through,

depart reality, and let imagination fill the void between

the unseen earth, and the white cloud-streaked sky.

But now I have business within the barn.

I must face my nemesis, struggle to escape my fate,

for I know what awaits me.

I must destroy – or be destroyed.

**Bernard Jacobs** © 2021

A River Runs Through It

Acrylic on canvas, 50 x 70 cms.

# A River Runs Through It

**Acrylic on canvas, 50 x 70 cms.**

A riot of gold and orange,
With flashes of green and silver,
Light glinting on the water,
Reflections wavering on the surface.

The same rain that feeds the river,
Has washed and cleansed the land,
Leaving colours rich and vibrant,
Intense in the cool clean air.

The river mirrors the cobalt sky,
Interrupted in the shingly shallows,
Sunlight glinting on the ripples,
Diamond flashes adorn the water.

Lush vegetation on the banks,
Birches and bushes in autumn robes,
Silver trunks punctuating the foliage,
Emerging from dark velvet shadow.

The river flows on undeterred,
Carving its curving path as it goes,
Soon to be adorned with gold,
As the birches lose their leaves.

**Fiona Hooper** © 2021

From an arch of aged stone
Where eyes like ours for years
Have stared along that precious beat,
Gazed upon that avenue of dazzling birch
And beyond, to that distant sheltered lea,
Where spring lambs play
And fatten on sweet verdant grass;

From that ancient span
See that blue cold river run through that
Quiet boulevard of coppered splendour,
Pleasure in the glint of sun on silver bark,
Watch the endless tide of gentle ripples forever
Brush the shaded tree lined bank, and melt;

And by that snake of rippled water
Above its bed of polished pebbles
Surrounded by fall's rural grandeur
A slender birch stands naked,
Barren bare and lifeless; in death,
Its beauty plain and haunting
Its thinnest twigs, like brittle bony arthritic fingers,
Stark against the blue tinged sky.

And hidden in that empty birks' strong
Shadow, deadly still, cold toes dipped
In silver dancing sun kissed ripples
A hungry heron crouched to hunt
That next precious meal.

In this pastoral, I hear
The cheering chirp of giggling finches
Hid amid the frail and lucent
Mandarin hued leafage;
Hear the kind breeze whisper through
The gently swaying foliage,
And in that warm autumnal air
Nose the fragrant scent of mossy birch.

And when the autumn idyll
Shifts to winter's certain chill,
And in life's madding frenzy
My busy mind is distant;
To this place by the river I will go;
And in the evening's fading sunlight
I will stand forever silent
And watch plump trout jump for flies.


**Martin Goldie**  © 2021

Prosper

# Gently Flows The River

**Oil on canvas board, 15 x 15 cms**

Snowbound in Winter's freeze,
With a surface of solid ice,
The river awakens come Spring,
Fed by melt water from above.

From frozen stillness and hibernation,
A trickle becomes a torrent,
With crystal clear, ice cold water,
Rushing from the crags on high.

The seasons change and Summer comes,
The rushing water calms and slows,
Burbling and babbling over the pebbles,
Playfully tumbling over hidden rocks.

Curving through the verdant land,
As Autumn steals into the valley,
The river moves silently now,
Diminished to a gentle flow.

Stubby trees stunted by the altitude,
Are mirrored in the now smooth water,
Its glassy surface undisturbed,
Waiting for the cycle to start anew.

**Fiona Hooper © 2021**

Softest lifeblood of the trees and earth,

Earth that nurtures the riverbank, like a mother.

Mother to all beasts who drink here,

Here where the water flows in peace.

Peace is her reward for her efforts,

Efforts of this bold and silent river.

River, feed your ecosystem well.

Well is he who bathes here, in solitude.

Solitude beneath green trees on green grass,

Grass that tickles the feet so gently.

Gently as the seductive touch of mother,

Mother carrying life, the essence of life.

Life itself owes so much to this place.

Place yourself on the quiet, patient shore.

Shore up your inner peace here.

Here lies the sacred vein of the infinite land.

**Ritesh Nigam © 2021**

# Cromer Pier

Oil on canvas, 40 x 80 cms.

# Cromer Pier

**Oil on canvas, 40 x 80 cms.**

It's the end of the day, a long, sun-filled, fun-filled day,
Walking the coast path, paddling in the foaming surf,
Children's sandcastles lying abandoned on the beach,
No match for the waves lapping at their sandy ramparts,
Nature smoothing its sandy canvas domain once more.

The kites have all been reeled in, the surf boards stowed,
Little crabs released from their confinement in buckets,
To be replaced by spades and beachcombing spoils -
Beautiful shells, bleached and sand-smoothed driftwood,
A crab's empty chalky carapace and a pretty little pebble.

As the light begins to fade, and the clouds take on a rosy hue,
The pier stands out in silhouette against the glowing sky,
Waiting for the lights that proclaim the evening's performance,
Attracting the holidaymakers for their nightly entertainment,
They gaze at Nature's beauty while strolling along the pier.

After a day in the refreshing and invigorating sea air,
Relax and reflect on the beauty of this serene scene,
The wet sand and shallow sea mirroring the sky's palette,
Washing away footprints and restoring its pristine glory,
Rest now and sleep, ready to do it all again tomorrow!

**Fiona Hooper** © 2021

The dark desolate castle casts reflection on the water as red sky
warns shepherds,
For this night the light has faded too soon as dark shadows stalk
the water's edge,
Foreboding sight silhouetted against pink night sky.

Still waters rolling and rippling meet the sky,
But quietist of all it comes to rest below castle wall
Where it creeps and crawls so not to disturb those eery shadows
That lurk on water as though waiting to pounce and slaughter.

Yet the sea knows it has more power than this dark pile of bricks
and mortar
That cast their spell on calm water, for if the sea should anger and
join forces with the sky
The storm would take away the rocks and that castle would die.

So they wait in solitude of harmony until the light falls over this
bay tranquil.

**Markey Mark Symmonds** © 2021

Hooper

## Sea Green

**Oil on canvas, 30 x 30 cms.**

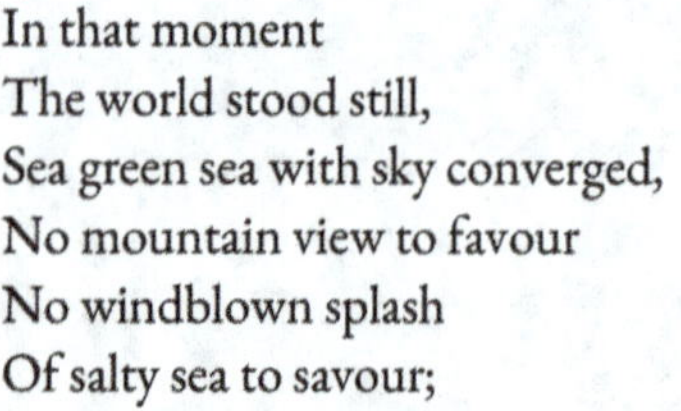

The silence of the mist dampens all sound,
While the waves roll on in endless inevitability,
Their cool greens and blues edged with white,
Colours to impart a sense of tranquillity.

The sea fret bestows an atmosphere of mystery,
Shape-shifting, enveloping, wrapping around us,
A damp, cool blanket of translucent moisture,
Rolling in, following the rhythm of the waves.

Mist formed by warm air over the chill waters,
Waiting for the breeze that creates the swells
And the reclusive sun to dissolve this obscuring veil,
To reveal its hidden treasures when the cloud dispels.

The fog-bound sea offers no clues to time of day,
And there will be no stars by which to steer,
We must rest and wait with enduring patience,
For this vaporous visitation to begin to clear.


**Fiona Hooper** © 2021

In that moment
The world stood still,
Sea green sea with sky converged,
No mountain view to favour
No windblown splash
Of salty sea to savour;

And as I stood on lichened rocks
Above an oft' deserted beach,
I felt the gentlest touch
Of soft warm breeze on tingling skin;

And in that silence,
Soaring high in salty air,
A startled eagle
Crying to the sky,
Fled inland to sheltered crags.

From my rock,
Smoothed by endless wind and tide,
On the edge of this wild land's end,
Immersed in that elusive slow time
We surely need,
I gazed across that calm virescent sea;

Where a winter storm's swirling snows
Released from purple louring clouds,
Float to earth from starless skies,
Land and melt on snow white sands
That glisten bright,
Between the machair and the swell;
Where Skye's black ragged form
Is risen from a shimmering sea;
Where doughty sea dogs
Home again from epic winter journeys,
A blaze of feather free and high,
Joyous in their azure space,
Dive with steel to pierce the sea;

In that quiet moment of perfection
In the moist briny air,
And like that hungry raptor,
I felt the slightest stir,
Sensed the brewing storms icy breath
Creep slowly from the west,

Watched dark clouds, blown
From wild Atlantic seas
Consume with stealth the massive sky,
Bar the light which pours,
Like liquid gold,
From that vast expanse of space,
Beyond those darkening skies;
That brilliant light,
Which warms this earth and
Fills our world with precious life.

As the storm's gloom gathered
And cast its bleak chill shadow
Upon the land and sea about me,
In the fast receding light,
I felt once more the random splash
Of salty sea refresh this aged weathered face.

And in that ocean's demented tempest
Livid lime seas frothed and splashed,
The wild wind wailed, and screaming
Frenzied waves, sped by wind and ocean's tide,
Rushed to where this land and sea are marked,
Where, in a thunderous deafening roar,
Those raging waters crashed
Upon this land's rocky coves and
Empty pristine white washed sands.

And when, at last, the storm blew through,
The eagle flew back on the hunt
And on this scene, quiet fell;
In that gorgeous calm,
Fragmented light, like pillars, fell,
Released from that eternal space
Beyond a broken sky of benign cloud;
In a miracle of sorts
Those shafts of empyrean light
Turned that sea green sea
Cyan blue.

**Martin Goldie** © 2021

# The Headland

Oil on canvas, 42 x 59.4 cms.

# The Headland

**Oil on canvas, 42 x 59.4 cms.**

What tales these rocks could tell,
If only they were able,
Of smugglers bold and contraband,
The stuff of legend and of fable.

Rugged rocks, strong and dark,
Tall cliffs resisting the sea's embrace,
Breakers thundering into dark caves,
Where brandy was hidden by the case.

Those ancient runners in their sailing ships,
Risking the hidden shards of granite,
Desperate to land their ill-gotten goods,
Could this be their last night on this planet?

The rascals are gone but the rocks remain,
Exposed to the Atlantic's full force,
Waves that have travelled the ocean's width,
Never deviating from their course.

Beside the headland, nestling close,
Sandy coves of golden sand,
Where white horses break on the beach,
Ridden by surfers, young and tanned.

Gulls soar on the salt laden breeze,
Making their nests on the steep cliff faces,
Raising their young and resting in safety,
In these high and inhospitable places.

Some say that on a moonlit night,
When the tides are high and the hour is late,
The spirits of those old rapskallions arise,
Aboard their ghostly ships, sailing to their fate.

**Fiona Hooper** © 2021

The hand of the Infinite carved out this cove.
Under cerulean sky and azure sea
It lifts my gaze to the horizon... senses far vast oceans...
Beyond, beyond where I can see.

The ebb and flow of timeless tides.
In harmony with rocky counterparts
Creates a haven warmed by sun and sand.
Without, within... the senses of my heart.

I can hear shanty songs: see smuggling ships.
Rich imagining of long lost tales
Of scattered wrecks, the seagulls screaming.
Backwards, forwards... wash of waves o'er broken sails.

I spy the grassy hill where lovers maybe climbed.
Once shared a secret kiss, or even three!
I trace it, curling round the headland, to this sheltered spot
Time and tide... now children playing carefree in the lee.

The coarse grass, yellow tipped by wind swept rush;
Contrast with coast moulded by the hand divine.
How can it be that earth gives up her beauty with such ease?
Simply complex contrast of the flow and line.

**Roz Ottery** © 2021

## Tracks On The Beach

Oil on board, 10 x 12 ins

# Tracks On The Beach

**Oil on board, 10 x 12 ins**

A new page, a blank canvas, an empty expanse,
The sand ironed flat with each rising tide,
All tracks and designs, circles and lines,
Erased without trace by the incoming waves.

Tracks made by swimmers on their daily visits,
Braving the waters, not missing a day,
Refreshing in summer and bracing in winter,
A great start to the day and then on their way.

The dog with its ball, paws churning the sand,
As it races and turns to reclaim its toy,
A break in the tracks as it runs through the surf,
Emerging again heading back whence it came.

On summer's warm days drawn by the ocean,
The families flock to the clean golden sands,
Tracks of all sizes, criss-crossing the shore,
Parents and children, and babies that crawl.

Surfers and kite boarders, horses and riders,
Sandpipers and gulls, crabs, worms and whelks,
Tracks large and small scripting their stories,
Made ephemeral by the waters of the incoming tide.

**Fiona Hooper** © 2021

Under an azure sky, beautiful blue

Blue borrowed by the sea below

Below from where I observe the shore

Shore lined by a serene track.

Track which was once filled with my footprints

Footprints now captured in this painting

Painting that I have mounted on my wall

Wall that I see everyday.

Everyday, painting takes me to the beach,

Beach that calms my mind,

Mind which vividly remembers the track on the beach.

**Ritesh Nigam** © 2021

# Rugged Sentinels

**Oil and silver leaf on canvas, 60 x 60 cms.**

Majestically they rise above the waves,
Imposing and implacable, old as time itself,
Resisting the salty spray and water's power,
These rugged sentinels keep their watch.

Dark walls dissected by ancient fissures,
Punctuated by splashes of gold and green,
Where life has taken root in shallow clefts,
Ekeing out its precarious existence.

Towering over the shimmering silvery sea,
Their crests provide the perfect vantage point,
They gaze out across the sun specked waves,
Witnessing all, yet seeing nothing.

On calm tranquil days, caressed by the sun,
Rocky facets illuminated and defined,
These unyielding bastions stand their ground,
To remain unchanged to eternity and beyond.

In man's short span these cliffs seem timeless,
But the solitary stacks that once were joined,
Now stand as evidence of their slow retreat,
Inevitable, inexorable, with imperceptible speed.

Measured in eons this change will continue,
But for now they endure, lofty and proud,
Crowned by Nature's rich glowing mantle,
Shielding the land from the force of the sea.

**Fiona Hooper © 2021**

Below the palest crescent moon,
Which shared a hazy sky
With fall's full broiling sun,
I lie, stretched out
On warm cropped grass,
Like a swollen lion asleep content
Below a baking Kenyan sun;

On this rarest of days,
In this harshest of lands, beguiled,
I lie, among green fading pastures,
Cooled by autumn's placid breezes
Upon a chequered rug of raucous
Gold and amber grasses,
Burning in that wondrous sun,
A fiery palette,
In my glowing face reflected,
And among scorched yellowed
Whispering grasses, I smell
The pungent scent of salty air,
On the gentlest North Atlantic breezes.

And from my earthy golden
Height, in silence undisturbed,
Distrait, I gaze,
West to endless dreamy blue,
Beyond dark sun starved cliffs,
And ancient rugged sentinels
Rising from the calm viridian
waters, in which their weathered
Granite form is mirrored,
Pointing, in their stance,
An accusatory finger to that
Hazy azure sky above me;

And far below, benign waves
Splash mutely on dark rugged rocks;
And in blue skies gannets stare,
And like an arrow loosed,
Dive from high to pierce
The cold blue shimmering sea.

Before the coming winter's storms
Swallow autumn's burning sun,
And livid winds taunt and numb
The veined cliffs vacant ledges;
When gentle puffins vibrant
Beaks are dulled, and fattened from
Their summer feast, they ready
For their winter absence.
Then, my work is done, then,
I may winter safe, dry within my
Turf roofed smoky black house.

But when, at last,
The welcome warmth of spring
Returns and usurps winter's
Long dark hailey nights; bestows
Again its kinder winds
Upon the cliffs and stacks of Kilda;
If spared my last departure,
I will stand again
Upon that tawny height,
And like the rugged sentinels before me,
wonder at those busy skies
Alive once more with flocks
Of shrieking birds,
Joyous in that frenzied
Show of recreational flying;
and, at this sight,
My simple life's grand purpose,
My reason now for being;
To rally the young men of Hirta,
And, as I once did,
In the distant mist of long missed years,
Scale the towering cliffs of Conachair,
Risk all to harvest life sustaining
Eggs and fulmar.


**Martin Goldie** © 2021

OOPER

# *Standing Proud*

**Mixed media on canvas, 16 x 16 ins.**

A single acorn, fallen here two centuries past,
Watered by the rain in the warm soft earth,
Nurtured by the sun as it emerged from the soil,
Purposefully reaching ever upward to the sky.

It survived being nibbled by hungry herbivores,
And branches wrested from it by Nature's fury,
It added height and girth with each passing year,
From seedling to sapling, growing tall and strong.

A slowly tapering trunk, branching as it rises,
Punctuated by rough grown callus' and scars,
Anchored and supported by far spreading roots,
Mirroring underground its spreading canopy.

From limb to branch, to a tracery of twigs,
A beautiful and interlaced dividing pattern,
It shows its graceful and delicate structure,
As it rests in the cool of the winter months.

Expectantly awaiting Spring's impending return,
The warmer, longer days as the Earth's axis tilts,
The cycle of life shifting dormant to active,
Waking the tree from its annual slumber.

The oak now senses a change in the air,
And will soon be clothed in its fresh green jacket,
A home for insects, birds, squirrels and bats,
And a shady retreat in the heat of Summer.

Having grown to majestic and stately maturity,
Standing proud and alone, in solitary splendour,
This ancient oak with gnarled and twisted limbs,
Is the perfect emblem of strength and endurance

**Fiona Hooper** © 2021

**(Song)**
Here I stand, tall proud and true,
'gainst the sky of milky blue
The wintry sun casts silver beams –
that seep in through my bark and seams
The freezing rain of winter's night
has given way to gentle light
I spread my limbs to catch each ray,
drink in the beauty of the day

*Chorus*
*And the memories of all the years*
*Sights I've witnessed, joys and tears*
*All these memories I do store*
*Deep inside this oaken core*

The two young lovers, lost in bliss,
under my branches stole a kiss
I felt no anger at the pains
when in my side they etched their names
They picnicked in my emerald shade,
years later on their children played
Among my limbs so broad and strong,
while robins trilled their merry song

*Chorus*

Then many years along life's road,
they'd visit still, their movement slowed
And sit on deck chairs on the grass,
and talk with me of good times past
I still remember that Autumn day,
with bitter wind and sky lead grey
She came alone, her body shrunk,
and leaned her head against my trunk

*Chorus*

Somehow I knew our time was past,
the seasons change they do not last
The sap within me rose in pain,
I never saw her face again
So here I stand in winter's chill,
my leafless branches stark and still
Once verdant fields stretch out below,
now covered white with sparkling snow.

*Chorus*

**Rosie Hodson** © 2021

Hooper

# White Horses In The Bay

**Oil on canvas, 40 x 40 cms.**

Where have they been,
What have they seen,
These racing white horses
Running their courses?

With creamy white foam,
Over the ocean they roam,
Across deep azure seas,
Blown by the breeze.

They run with the tide,
On a white-knuckle ride,
No master have they,
No hand to obey.

Watery hooves pounding,
Leaping and bounding,
Breaking against stacks,
Forging new tracks.

Corralled in the bay,
They tumble and play,
Stirring up sand,
As they advance on the land.

It's been a long run,
Under stars and the sun,
But here on the beach,
Is a far as they reach.

**Fiona Hooper** © 2021

Brown rocks emerge after every swell that rushes over and around

decaying all the surface washing it of colour breaking down.

Every minute mineral until all that is left

is dark solid rocks that refuse to move to be shifted.

Standing strong but decaying day by day from constant wear.

Then as the tide peels back and the nights fall

all that it hears is the whisper of those waves tormenting it

daring it to split and crack into smaller pieces as it did once when headland.

But the rock knows that if it cracks it will surely perish and wash away with the sea

The rock instead stands mighty in the swell of the sea hard and devoid of light

just staying in the fight day and night

as the tide rushes in and out in spite.

Trying to alter the seascape forever. To be recovered at first light.

**Markey Mark Symmonds** © 2021

F HOOPER

# New Beginnings

**Oil and gold leaf on canvas, 40 x 40 cms.**

Moving through the forest, on a soft carpet of leaves,
Under the filigree canopy of dense woven twigs,
A small clearing is found where sunbeams reach down,
And there at the back, at the side of the track,
A sapling quite small, not yet five feet tall.

With but a few years of growing, bark smooth and grey,
It was born of the mast that tumbled from up high,
That small shiny nut in its prickly armour, sprouting,
Reaching down in the earth and up to the sky,
The tiniest tree in the forest, is now over knee high.

In the shadow of giants, trees many decades its senior,
Sheltered from the storms and blistering heat,
With each new branch it reaches ever upwards,
Seeking the warmth and the light of a life-giving sun,
Ascending from the shade where its life was begun.

Like a child it is innocent of the ways of the woods,
With its fresh young leaves in serrated lime green,
Where the moth lays her eggs underneath, unseen,
A readymade larder for her annual brood,
Waiting to hatch for fresh and still growing food.

The beech is the Queen of our British trees,
And our sapling merely a princess in waiting,
It'll be many years yet till she can take her crown,
When her branches mingle with those of her peers,
And her own beech mast will go tumbling down.

**Fiona Hooper** © 2021

Our planet is in crisis
We humans are to blame
No thoughts about tomorrow
Without a sense of shame
We trample fragile flowers
And chop down countless trees
We're lawless and we're thoughtless
We do what the hell We please
Orangutans in Borneo
Have few trees left to climb
We're not concerned with where they'll go
We haven't got the time
Those ocean-dwelling turtles
Being strangled every day
By the plastic rings round beer cans
That we casually throw away
Our coral reef is dying
From the toxins in the sea
Entire species in decline
That's down to you and me!
Our eco system's struggling
And to humankind it's linked
Mammals, birds and butterflies
Some are now extinct!
I fear for every rainforest
From Borneo to the UK
An area the size of Paris Is demolished every day!
The trees supply the oxygen
Which gives us air to breathe
In felling them, you're killing us!
Why are we so naive?
Plastics along with oil spills
Will our race just never learn?
If we don't act now, it will be too late
And polluted tides will turn...

**Yvonne Ugarte** © 2021

# Venice Dreams

**Oil and ink on canvas, 50 x 50 cms.**

A mysterious mist, a tender cocoon of vapour,
Soft and enveloping, shrouding the city at dawn,
Pearlescent droplets reflecting the roseate glow,
As the sun awaits its appointed hour to be born.

The cool moist miasma, rising from the water,
Blanketing, muffling, and deadening sound,
Masks a distant voice from an unseen source,
From where did it come and where is it bound?

Water laps lazily at the ancient wooden posts,
Responding to the barely perceptible swell,
Sheltered from the ocean in this shallow lagoon,
Where traders and merchants elected to dwell.

The quiet engine's thrum of some passing boat,
Cautiously crossing through the shifting veils,
Nosing slowly forwards, scanning the silver cloud,
Full knowing in slowness that safety prevails.

Soon now the sun will ascend from its sleep,
The light will gleam on the tall, gilded towers,
The mist metamorphose into a beautiful city,
Venice dreams giving way to its daylight hours.

**Fiona Hooper** © 2021

Hazy whispers of silhouetted brilliance;

Structural plenitude etched with fragrant shadows.

A drooping mist scrubs those lines, frontiers and rooted
foundations,

Evoking a silent majesty that seeps –

Sleeps within a cracking, glorious fog.

Receptive. Speechless; fixed in a central perspective the longing
eye casts

A teary look. Hooked

Away from its squirming travels by this ripple of emerging
order.

Projected passions and bottled thoughts,

Those dreams that swirl within, split

And aimlessly disperse, are refracted

Into a hopeful illumination,

Carved and smoothed by each point, outline and jutting pole –

Every border, every contour a watchful prism,

Tunnelling chaotic cares into a discernable vision.

**Oscar Nicholson** © 2021

## Last Of The Snow

Oil on canvas board, 13 x 18 cms

# Last Of The Snow

**Oil on canvas board, 13 x 18 cms**

The last of the snow lingers at the edge of the trees,
Lying in the shadows hidden from the sun's warm rays,
A reminder of winter's glistening crystalline freeze,
And those busy, boisterous, activity filled days.

Distant faint echoes of voices that hang in the air,
Memories of the cries of delight from young and old,
The swish of the skis and the rush of a toboggan,
And the shouts of snow-boarders brave and bold.

With the passing of the snow, and the warmth of the sun,
The valley becomes a haven of peace and tranquillity,
With air clean and pure, and light sharp and bright,
Nature makes haste in this short season of fertility.

The calls of the crows which bounced off the snow,
Are now muted, absorbed by the pasture revealed,
The valley provides summer grazing for wildlife,
Come down to feed from the high mountain pass.

Nestled under towering peaks topped by icy crowns,
Below the sheer sides with their lavender shadows,
The wildlife reclaims this land as its own,
And man seldom ventures to these summer plateaus.

Spring turns into summer, the seasons are short,
The young of the elk and the white-tailed deer,
Grow swiftly building muscles and strength,
Nourished by the foliage which flourishes here.

Come autumn the clouds will be pregnant with snow,
The days will contract and the nights feel chill,
The animals sense that it's time to move on,
And man will be waiting for the next winter thrill.

Under the beautifully distant blue azure sky

Sky with serene patchy clouds tattooed to sit high

High it sits magnificent to my eyes

Eyes that fly to the mountains capped white

White is the snow covering three crests right

Right as it drops to the dark wood's sight

Sight of the emerald's motionless trance

Trance drawing attention to the winding dance

Dance of crossing snakes through the bushes aligned

Aligned to densely forests opening up to trees shrined

Shrined is every tree, dark thickets to protect

Protect them from the mountain's conquering impact

Impact of poking noses through the sky of frosty whiff

Whiff that I can't sniff as I am standing here stiff

Stiff in front of this mounted painting that I know

Know that it's showing us the last of the snow.

**Ritesh Nigam**  © 2021

PHOOPER

# Splash Of Light

**Oil and gold leaf on canvas, 40 x 40 cms.**

Deep in the ageless forest, a tranquil and secretive place,
Air dense with the aromatic velvety softness of the shadows,
The light is filtered by a mosaic of infinite greens and golds,
Glinting on insects and dust motes as they dance in the glade,
Riding the gentle air currents of this sheltered private world.

Beneath the soaring canopy, on the forest floor below,
The scents of warm earth and damp leaves saturate the air,
Heady with the redolent fragrance of ancient memories,
A comforting and calming balm with hints of soft green moss,
Timeless and enduring, caressing the senses with peace.

Recessed amongst these majestic and enduring living pillars,
Is the wonderful and beguiling mystery of emergent new life,
Resplendent in its coat of golden leaves, radiant and glowing,
The sapling pushes upwards, away from the moist forest floor,
A splash of light illuminating hues of fresh vibrant lemon.

In this verdant sanctuary it will follow the cycles of nature,
Growing, resting, striving towards the light far above,
Until its branches mingle and meld with those of its elders,
Nurturing and protecting the myriad wildlife of the forest,
Taking its place in this fragile and precious realm.

**Fiona Hooper** © 2021

A burst of oxygen fills my lungs
as I take a walk in the outdoors
The soothing sounds of leaves rustling in the breeze
As the sun shows through the luminescent green

The feel of the fern as it caresses my feet
containing tiny drops of dew as the sun shines through
With arms of light stretching directly from the sky
Casting a glow with orange and yellow hues

The rich brown shades against the sea of greens
Create the perfect skin tone for the many trees
The giant stems heading towards the heavens above
Their flag like branches wave in the wind's up tempo beat

Fingers follow the shape of a tree bark
Feeling every ridge, valley, swirl and curve
Learning its unique wooded fingerprint
That adds to the surrounding autumn forest scene

The ochre and umber colors create the earth tones
Upon which the sun spreads its warmth through filtered light
It is the perfect setting for a beautiful masterpiece
Where one's soul continues beyond the dimensions of space and
time

Nothing beats an experience in nature
One that is enjoyed without any filters
so please, come and join me
in the choreographed dance of the wind and trees.

**Aliberry SP** © 2021

# Light And Shade

Oil on board, 10 x 12 ins

# *Light And Shade*

**Oil on board, 10 x 12 ins**

A quiet retreat, tranquil and secluded,
Sleepily blanketed in a gentle hush,
I set my easel at the water's edge,
Cushioned on grass, green and lush.

The deep dark depths of the inky pool,
With its archipelago of living islands,
Floating serenely on the glassy water,
A deft touch needed by the artist's hand.

A shaft of sun breaks across the bank,
And light illuminates a vivid green,
Be careful now – I must take my time,
I really need to keep my colours clean.

The music of nature surrounds me,
A gentle, hypnotic murmur of life,
Mayflies dart around and hover,
Settling happily on brush and knife.

The air is heavy with afternoon warmth,
The sheep graze lazily in the pasture,
I need to portray this mellow calm,
Of colour and tone I must be a master.

Shards of light, reflections on the water,
And a decision must now be made,
How bright the lights, how dark the darks,
So vital to depict the light and shade!

**Fiona Hooper** © 2021

In the primal peace
Of a dawning glade,
The new sun splashed
Its welcome light, upon
The slowly waking
Shore of a tree lined
Still black pond;
A soot choked city's
Sweet breathed pearl,
Where fox and roe
In night's blue moonlight
Slake;
Where, in the new day's
Golden light, flaming damsels
Busy flit and pleasing breezes
Barely ripple
The deep dark water's
Glassy surface;
Where mirrored mallards
Guard intently,
And cryptic waters,
Softly kissed
By the frailest slivers
Of shivering silver,
Glisten gently,
Among the cheering hue
Of bowing birch
and fragrant lilies;
And the shrill
Staccato vocalise
Of a skittish blackbird's
Insistent reprise; and hidden
In the glades dark shadows
Plump thrush perch
On wet dewed branches,
Anxious for that maiden flight;

In that dappled clearing,
A gasping town's
Breathing lung,
Light and shade
Stage their drama,
And in a steamy summer's
Precious slow time,
With little purpose,
Summer lovers lie forever;
In their moment,
Lie in concert,
In flitting peace,
Lie reflective,
Gazing skyward,
Below a different sky,
Before that purring black
Lily pond, they lie,
On a cushioned bed of naked,
Sweetly scented lemon grasses;
In that eternal moment,
Wrapped in fragile dreams
Of what time may reveal,
They drift,
Enchanted in the dreamy light,
Below a hot sun burning,
Sun kissed bodies tingling,
Fingers lightly touching,
Futures quietly pondering;
And quiet in that tacit flight,

Hear whispered breath touch
Still black waters,
Breathe deep the glade's lush air.

**Martin Goldie** © 2021

## The Old Hen House

Oil on board, 10 x 12 ins

# The Old Hen House

**Oil on board, 10 x 12 ins**

Tucked away against the hedge,
Forgotten and neglected,
Windows opaque with grime and dirt,
Hiding the darkness within.

Sunlight rakes across the leaky roof,
Where once a proud rooster crowed,
Waking all from their morning slumbers,
Weekday or weekend, it was all the same to him.

There used to be clucking and flapping,
The raucous squawk of an egg song after laying,
A quiet rustling in the dark of night,
As the hens slept and dreamt therein.

There'd be consternation at a fox on the prowl,
And excitement at fresh peelings, cabbage and grain,
Clean straw bedding and a carpet of shavings,
With fresh brown eggs to be collected every day.

This old wooden house on its rusted wheels,
Once busy and vibrant stands silent now,
Where spiders and bugs were once a tasty snack,
The cobwebs hang, wreathlike, undisturbed.

**Fiona Hooper** © 2021

The farmstead stands abandoned

With no more crops to sow

A haven, now, for nature

Where abundant wild flowers grow

But nestled there among them

Stands a henhouse, paint like new

The wooden roof staves off the rain

Only sunshine filters through

On the grass beside it

Lies the proof of life before

Scattered feathers, husks of corn

And a presence by the door

Phantom eggs fill empty nests

And a cockerel softly crows

Ghostly hens heard clucking low

But are they real? Who knows ?

**Yvonne Ugarte** © 2021

Kingsgate Bay, Kent

Oil on board, 12 x 16 ins

# *Kingsgate Bay, Kent*

**Oil on board, 12 x 16 ins.**

These ancient towering white cliffs,
Glowing golden in the lowering sun,
That now rise high above the waters,
Were once submerged beneath the waves,
Formed millennia past when time was young,
The lasting legacy of primordial plankton.

Their chalky form makes them vulnerable,
By tide and weather they are sculpted,
Where once a vast plateau stretched far,
Now a ragged coastline borders the waves,
With carved arches and tidal caverns,
Always changing, always receding.

The glassy waters of the sheltered bay,
Mirror the cliffs and cerulean skies,
Reflecting the beauty of this coastal idyll,
With its timeless and glorious splendour,
A place of peace, a haven of tranquillity,
A feast for the eyes and food for the soul.

**Fiona Hooper** © 2021

Lonely figures black shadows against the

yellow sand and chalk of Kent cliffs.

Where no happy little bluebirds fly.

Sheer height says you can't come in,

Yet it surveys all the sea and maritime folk know

this island they have stumbled across

as there lays a symbol, a barrier, do not cross.

Yet the calmness of water creeping on beach's sand

as the shadows walk hand in hand

and white foam ripples up the sand

they know they landed in the promised land.

The cliffs reach for the sky teasing boats

never asking why yet signalling home

for travellers afar mesmerized

by that white chalk rise.

And shadows keep watching for bluebirds to fly

Vera Lynn's words echo and die

did she tell a lie or will those birds one day spy

before two lovebirds decide to fly.

**Markey Mark Symmonds** © 2021

## Estuary Reflections

Acrylic on canvas, 40 x 60 cms

# *Estuary Reflections*

**Acrylic on canvas, 40 x 60 cms.**

Gazing out across the lustrous water,
Serenaded by a curlew's haunting call,
I revel in the beauty of this lonely place,
And the evening light before night's fall.

The sun still plays on the distant bank,
A patchwork landscape of umber and green,
Under a moody sky with gossamer clouds,
Glowing with warmth from a sun unseen.

Here the salty ocean meets with the river,
Changing with the ebbs and flows of the tide,
Rocky fingers reaching out from the shore,
As though to bridge this watery divide.

With winter comes the clamour of geese,
And ducks spooked by a hunting harrier,
The wintering wildfowl who stop to feed,
Find this water a refuge, not a barrier.

For them the mudflats are a rich resource,
With shellfish, crabs, fish and worms,
A source of food to raise their young,
Until they all fly north when Spring returns.

But now the light is dwindling fast,
And dusk is changing my perceptions,
I must leave for now this gentle shore,
With fond memories of estuary reflections.

**Fiona Hooper** © 2021

The blanketed night fades and a clear picture becomes unveiled
While the sun slowly blossoms lighting up the morning sky
If I could paint upon the surface of the estuary and hold a mirror
up against its rays
It would be a perfect reflection of what my heart does whenever I
think of you and I

The fluffy and wispy clouds saturated with a soft orange and
golden glow
Others create a ribbon that spans the bluish-grey canvas
The puffiness reminds me of how full my heart has come to be
The pride I felt and still feel once I said yes to making you mine

The mix of fresh water and the saltiness of the sea
Mimics the ecosystem that our love has come to be
A unique blend containing the right amount of salinity
Just enough to season our lives for years to eternity

As the clouds move revealing more patches of blue
The incoming light stamps the sky's scene across the water
beneath
An announcement of an approaching sunrise or impending rain
A reminder to hold you close no matter what path our lives may
take

Just as this place remains home to multiple species of life
Surrounded by lush vegetation and cool, crisp air
My hope is that our love will continue to survive
Leaving lasting impressions on those we meet everywhere

**Aliberry SP** © 2021

Hooper

# Sunshine After The Rain

**Oil on board, 12 x 10 ins**

It was one of those days, changeable,
We ran for cover as the raindrops fell,
Across the meadow and back inside,
Accompanied by the ground's moist smell.

We stayed at the open door, waiting,
Listening to the steady rhythm of the rain,
The thrumming of the falling drops,
Beating on the window pane.

The trees stood staunchly, dripping,
Sheltering the ground below,
Their leaves a panoply of tiny brollies,
Not stopping but slowing the water's flow.

At last the clouds were breaking, lifting,
And the rain was coming to an end,
It had washed off all the dust and grime,
The heavy shower was all but stemmed.

As the sun came out of hiding, glowing,
The colours all so clean and bright,
Glistening leaves glinting like diamonds,
A world bathed in rain now bathed in light.

The trees are changing colour, slowly,
As daylight hours start to wane,
But for now we'll enjoy the greens and golds,
Here in the sunshine after the rain.

**Fiona Hooper** © 2021

There is something that we all need to understand.
Understand why this painting is portraying a stand.
Stand that screams of something so loud.
Loud amidst the modern horns yet producing an ineffective sound.
Sound of wind I hear through the trembling of the leaves
Leaves of green, yellow and orange with its beauty it deceives.
Deceives me as I get lost in all these shades of green
Green grass that stretches all the way to meet serene
Serene calm sky with trace of white reflecting from the clouds.
Clouds to be felt but mostly not noticed by the common crowds
Crowds that know of only cement and concrete jungle ahead.
Ahead of what is more cement where all the green is dead
Dead are the ones who have not noticed this world so true
True to make you believe in a world that's green for you
You and me who fail to understand the rules of this land
Land of green is here portraying for us to understand and take a stand.

**Ritesh Nigam** © 2021

## Country Lane

Oil on board, 10 x 12 ins

## *Country Lane*
**Oil on board, 10 x 12 ins**

Nestled in the valley below the moors,
This peaceful and bucolic scene awaits,
A view unchanged for decades past,
Where time passes at a slower rate.

Shadows rake across the lane,
Fording the grass and climbing the hedge,
Striping the surface with light and shade,
Changing course as they meet each edge.

The lowing of cattle ready for milking,
And the songs of skylarks overhead,
The distant bleat of sheep on the moors,
Tell tales of the life that lies ahead.

The farm has seen many generations,
The custodians of this beautiful land,
Knowledge passed from father to son,
Methods old and new at their command.

The hedgerows are a haven for wildlife,
The moors home to grouse and heather,
Let's not forget how fragile is this land,
We need to preserve and protect it forever.

**Fiona Hooper** © 2021

Each road leads onwards towards a new horizon
And none may guess the journey or gauge the heavy load.
The current curves and bumps pose challenges for every traveller...
For only one pair of feet can travel this whole road.

Here pleasant English fields, surrounding a small hamlet.
The single, pale warm day helps steps be light and sure.
So pleasant in cool shade of this one moment
So palpable the silence; sweet and pure.

What will that next turn bring? What challenge waiting?
This fluidity of life... This captured scene.
For every turn is a new adventure for each pilgrim
And each age has changed the picture that has been.

For maybe once, here, land girls toiled to feed a country,
While Messerschmitts flew past: this sky to streak.
For those that walked this landscape in the war years,
Different scenes would manifest and speak.

So capture now this scene in autumn cream and orange.
Resplendent moment nature and peace blend.
Feed tranquillity to eyes that know what's given.
Dwell a while, 'afore our own sad story ends.

**Roz Ottery** © 2021

## Sheep May Safely Graze

Oil on board, 10 x 12 ins

# Sheep May Safely Graze

**Oil on board, 10 x 12 ins**

In this green and fertile land, with pastures of lush grass,
Away from the noise and pollution of traffic and town,
The sheep meander calmy, quietly cropping as they go,
Safe in their field bounded by hedge and fence.

No more the mighty wolf and bear prowling the land,
And the sheep graze in relative peace and tranquillity,
But instincts still remain strong below the surface,
Easing the work of the shepherd and his dogs.

As a stranger approaches, striding along the track,
They raise their heads to gaze with bemused curiosity,
Then returning to the essential business of grazing,
Satisfied that the potential danger has passed.

Their wild predators are long gone from this populous isle,
But now they face new threats – rustlers, diminishing space,
And a climate which veers between increasing extremes.
Is this world truly a place where sheep may safely graze?

**Fiona Hooper** © 2021

Timeless, this pastoral I witness,

Without the heinous appurtenance

Which now belong and spoil many rural vistas.

And stood within that field's lush silence,

Deep into my burning soul, I breath the acres

Of shimmering verdure stretched before me,

Embrace the landscapes shifting rhythms,

Feel it slowly wake from nature's tempestuous fury,

Evidenced in dark remnants of that recent storm,

Scudding in that sky blue sky.

And from those rushing clouds, a final fall of steamy rain,

Released from that departing tempest,

Spitting daggers on verdant meadows,

Which edge a dark river's flowing waters,

Where large frogs shuffle in soaking grasses,

Relieved to miss the final fatal stab

Of a hungry wader's deadly beak.

In that quiet wake, from hidden nests

to cheerful skies, larks rise in sublime song

And feel again the burn of sun

Dry dripping feather.

And, from a sleepy rustic hamlet,

Snuggled cosy on a wooded rise,

With a haunting melancholy,

The feeble cry of a restive dog

Lingered long in lazy air, touched

Like a lone bugle's last post,

Fused in blue fragrant wood smoke,

Drifted loathe down jade hedged fields,

To a dapple green leafy oak wood,

Where blazing squirrels once more gather,

Finches flit and siskins sing, where

Butterflies float on gentle wind

And a woodpecker's hypnotic rattle

Echoes through the bowery forest.

And in that sun drenched woods

Mottled hollows, fragrant mentha and vivid

Purple foxglove, entice awakened bees

With a feast of pleasing nectar.

In the short-lived peace of that

Hot summer's slumberous lull,

Before succeeding storms prevail

And quiet nature's exquisite choir,

Before the short black night

Casts shadow on that quiet meadow,

There, below pale quiet skies,

Brimming with great puffy clouds,

That mirror bright frothing waves

Treading heaven's vast blue ocean,

A flock of gravid ewes

Warmed by gentle breeze,

Graze safely on sweet meadow grass.

**Martin Goldie** © 2021

Hooper

# Light On The Moors

**Oil on canvas, 30 x 30 cms**


Escaping from the city with its confining walls,
To wide open spaces and the freedom to breathe,
The freedom to think in the quiet and solitude,
To wander at will, to roam wild and free.

Fill your lungs with the clean refreshing air,
Feel the oxygen coursing round your veins,
Let the breeze blow away tension and stress,
Till only deep, calm tranquillity remains.

Watch the clouds scudding o'er the landscape,
Casting shadows that slide across the land below,
The sun playing games of hide and seek,
Its searching beams making the moorland glow.

Dissected by branching valleys and streams,
And home to grouse, merlin, rabbit and sheep,
They each find their niche on the open moor,
In the heather and sedge, or in the valley steep.

The silence heightens the sounds of nature,
Far away from the city's relentless noise,
A curlew's plaintive call and the whistle of a harrier,
Are sounds the happy wanderer here enjoys.


**Fiona Hooper** © 2021

Tween day and night, blue grey mist swirls,
In pale half light, it twists and curls
Above the lime green undulating
Valleys where the fog lies waiting
Burnished copper trees stand guard,
The peaceful emptiness regard,
And forging through between their boughs
A dark ravine of shrubland ploughs
Spreading, branching o'er the land
Like veins upon a giant hand,
Palm outstretched towards the light,
The ghostly film of misty white
That separates the earth and sky
Who knows what buried secrets lie
Beneath the rolling gentle plains
As Autumn dies and winter reigns

Who knows if many years ahead
This misty vista may instead
Be splattered on by vast estates
Of boxy homes with fancy gates
And shopping malls, ice skating rinks
The restaurant chains with food and drinks
And neon signs so over bright
Completely mask the moorland light
But for the present peace still reigns
O'er this most secret of domains
Untouched, unclaimed, it thrills and awes
Lit only by the pale light on the moors.


**Rosie Hodson** © 2021

HOOPER

## *Snow Capped*

**Oil on canvas, 30 x 30 cms**

Remote, bleak and barren,
Exposed to the full force of the biting wind,
These mountains wear their snowy mantles,
Glowing coldly in the winter light.

A waterfall suspended as an icy flow,
Waiting for the months to pass
Till its release from enforced inertia,
Reborn as a gushing spate of melted ice.

Rich russets from Autumn's faded leaves,
Contrast sharply with the cold whiteness,
A reminder of the colour that fills these valleys
When the winter releases its bitter grip.

The violet greyness of the leaden skies,
Bears down with heavy burden of ice and snow,
Curtailing further the short winter days,
Blocking the sun's meagre watery rays.

Wildlife seeks the bare shelter of the valleys,
Or retreats to burrows and nests,
Avoiding the abrasive ice laden wind,
Which scours and blasts this wild land.

Life is tough in this unforgiving world,
With freeze and thaw breaking even the rocks,
But in spite of that I love this place,
In all its harsh and rugged beauty.

**Fiona Hooper** © 2021

Feelings, snow-capped, kept under wraps of thin ice
with a boundary fence of warning signs,
keep you at my edges never knowing
the slightest pressure would crack me wide open
Never knowing I keep my dark side away from your light
To keep glacial flow watertight
Preventing a torrent with too much momentum
to be dammed leaving me damned
When it destroyed you.

I stay muted. Winter landscape against winter sky
Impervious to your efforts to traverse the climb
But if you could wait for me long enough
for winter to pass into spring.
Await my blue skies and a natural thawing.
Await as I awaken from this winter hibernation
this locking down of senses keeping me senseless
keeping what life is left in my soul out of the cold,
protected,
until hope warms my frozen slopes
germinating new growth.
a burst of colour
covering me in layers more welcoming

On that day, you can make the climb
and the view of our shared horizon
will be worth gazing upon.
The snow caps will retract
And we will dance in sunshine
The balancing of nature
we can neither pre-empt nor simulate
But the change of seasons is worth the wait.

**Skylar J Wynter** © 2021

# Resting In The Shade

Oil on canvas board, 13 x 18 cms

# *Resting In The Shade*

**Oil on canvas board, 13 x 18 cms**

The afternoon heat,
Molten gold streaming down,
Trapped in the valley,
Remorseless, inescapable.

As the mercury climbs
Even insects fall quiet,
Their lazy drone ceases,
Too tiring in the stifling heat.

Relentless rays beat down,
The air burning and dry,
The world is at a lull,
Waiting, hoping for relief.

It's siesta time,
Too hot for working,
Heat haze shimmers
Creating a watery mirage.

The zephyr on the hills
Doesn't penetrate down here,
Its cooling caress reserved
For those higher levels.

Colours rich and vivid,
Heightened by the sun,
Deep, dark, inky shade,
Crouches under dense foliage.

Lethargic cattle, motionless,
Their grazing interrupted,
Silhouetted in the shadows,
Thankful for small respite.

Drowsily they chew the cud,
A tail swishes gently,
Patiently they wait for evening,
While resting in the shade.

**Fiona Hooper** © 2021

The blazing sun was relentless
Stretches of its molten beams spread across the land
The green in its path was tinted with a fiery glow
just shy of the space beneath the tree

A few plants wilt in search of shade
The scorching sun mocks us all standing in its path
Once playing peek a boo in the early morn
no longer hiding behind clouds

The dog and I after running in the field
finally seek shelter under the sole tree
We lay upon a small bed of grass
Creating a spring like effect against my back

We are canopied by the magnificent broad leaves
while the sunlight arrows try to find a space to come through
Each leaf marked with a network of prominent veins
similar to blood vessels which transport the vital nutrients we
need

In the shade I can hear
the wind rustling the overhead leaves
Even the birds sing along
creating their own tunes in the breeze

a strong but old tree with deep roots
Home for the animals
A place of protection from unknown enemies
and for us, a place to rest briefly

I take a moment and look at the distant trees
And the horizon studded with mountain peaks
the sky filled with clouds lazily moving by
To accept that mother nature left this tree here alone
and knows why

In a few more minutes, the dog and I will go home
An end to another day spent outdoors
We are thankful for the shade the tree provides
it stands as the pillar, a place of safety
And a reminder of its resiliency

**Aliberry SP** © 2021

## Of Sand And Sea

Oil on board, 10 x 12 ins

# Of Sand And Sea

**Oil on board, 10 x 12 ins**

Here, at the edge of the land, at the margins of beach and sea,
With waves rolling in from far away, is where I love to be.
Sea breezes and fresh salt air, re-energising and relaxing,
Rejuvenate my soul, make me oblivious of time elapsing.

The tall red cliffs at my back, from which the sand was formed,
At the mercy of the ocean, waves driven by tides and storms,
Majestic they stand yet inevitably and slowly they crumble,
With the power of the pounding waves, gradually they tumble.

I love to feel the fresh clean air blowing through my hair,
The salty taste on my lips and feeling so alive and aware,
The water glinting like diamonds, digging my toes in the sand,
Looking for treasure washed up on this golden strand.

Shells and sea washed glass, pieces of salt-bleached driftwood,
Holding the same enchantment as they did during childhood,
Seaweed tumbling, torn from its moorings on the seabed below,
The sound of breakers on sand, sucking back in the undertow.

These big skies above me with gulls soaring high in the briny air,
Their grace on the wing and mastery of flight beyond compare,
I listen to their plaintive piercing cries as I stroll on this sandy shore,
The wonder and beauty of this place keep me coming back for more.

**Fiona Hooper** © 2021

Receding tide cleanses each grain of sand,
each square inch clean as if untouched by foot or hand.
Leaving the beauty of sparse blank canvas
ready to rewrite life day after day.
Rain or shine this beach this bay
becomes a storytelling tale of failure and glory.

Yet even that blank clean fresh surface leaves traces of residue,
trickles of life that came before.
The elixir that pools and ripples to remind you of what came before.
Of what fails to recede even after the stampede
the turmoil of shifting soil.
Veins in life still gaping, gasping for air;
to lay bare the hurt that ripples and bubbles behind that façade.
Exposing that deep-seated renegade that cuts with a rusty blade.

Then the despair of the sea drowns out the call of the air
the freshness untainted by the turmoil that left its spoils
and yet so intertwined are the wind and sea
as are tears and the life we breathe
that constant in out renewal of lines
removal of signs until the end of time.

**Markey Mark Symmonds** © 2021

## Reclaimed By Nature

Oil on board, 10 x 12 ins

# *Reclaimed By Nature*

**Oil on board, 10 x 12 ins**

Hidden away at the end of the pond,
Lost and forgotten from another era,
Camouflaged with mosses and ferns,
The sluice gate sits, idle and overgrown.

Always damp in this shady corner,
Its mechanism long since rusted solid,
No more will it control the water's flow,
In this once cherished garden pond.

Patiently it waits, with its gate ajar,
A resting place for darting dragonflies,
With shimmering blue green wings,
Bright jewels against the old dark wood.

Surrounded by every shade of green,
From fresh, bright, softly plump mosses,
To deep, dark and mysterious recesses,
The lush and verdant growth abounds.

Inhale the moist earthiness of the air,
Redolent with damp wood and water,
Hear the rustling of the leaves overhead,
At the gentle touch of an unseen breeze.

The old wood turning a greenish hue,
Ironwork rusting, timber slowly rotting,
Disappearing behind a growing curtain,
Gradually being reclaimed by nature.

**Fiona Hooper** © 2021

Down at the end of the overgrown field

Stands a well that's neglected, forlorn

It's hidden amongst a wild rainbow of flowers

And its bricks are all crumbling and worn

But the well hides a secret No humans can see

Nature knows, but she won't tell

The bucket is rusted but used every year

By a thrush: her brood's raised in that well

Insects take refuge between the cracked stones

Butterflies dance high above

To us, it may seem like an old, broken well

But it's bursting with life and with love.

**Yvonne Ugarte** © 2021

H Hooper

# From Forest To Meadow

**Oil and gold leaf on canvas, 40 x 30 cms**

In amongst the columns of the solid trunks,
Under the dense green canopy of needles,
I breathe the sharp, refreshing fragrance,
Allowing its resinous warmth to soothe me,
Working unseen to calm my mind and soul.

The embrace of the enveloping moist air,
The closeness of shadow and soft light,
The roughness of grey bark under my fingers,
And a deep soft carpet cushioning my steps,
As I wander in nature's hallowed beauty.

The trees emanate peace and tranquillity,
They have learned patience and humility,
And will share their secrets and connection
With those souls who are willing to listen,
And to experience the quiet of calmness.

Walking between the dark silhouetted trunks,
As though passing through life's doorways,
I come once more to the edge of this sanctuary,
To the warm golden glow of an open sky,
And the warmth of sunlight warming my skin.

After the comforting stillness of the forest,
The meadow seems to abound with life,
Tall grasses weaving and gently whispering,
A foil for the soaring song of the larks above,
And I know my life is richer for the trees.

**Fiona Hooper** © 2021

Forest to meadow Lost in this colossal forest for days

Days traveling to find a prudent safe place

Place that will shepherd me out of here

Here where no soul can exist out there

There I see the mellow meadow grounds

Grounds stretching to the oblivion and back

Back to my despairing self for now

Now that I found a hefty hope to track

Track myself to the swirling waters nearby

Nearby as they flow when meadow's around

Around I see the whole world changing

Changing as I leave this perilous ground

Ground thyself to the meadow in sight

Sight with last of the forest ghetto

Ghetto that marks the forest fringes

Fringes portrayed as 'Forest to meadow'

**Ritesh Nigam** © 2021

## Woodland Gold

Oil on canvas, 40 x 80 cms

# *Woodland Gold*

**Oil on canvas, 40 x 80 cms**

Ancient woods, mysterious and ethereal,
Draped in a soft and hazy blue miasma,
Evoking feelings of awe and excitement,
Yet full of the peace of the stately trees.

At first apparently hushed and silent,
Yet alive with myriad small sounds of life,
The crackling and rustling of movement,
As leaves are disturbed and settle again.

Deer emerge from nowhere, wraithlike,
Perfectly camouflaged, with silent steps,
They blend into the shadows and the mist,
Out of sight but watching all the while.

Squirrels climb the smooth grey trunks,
Searching out their concealed larders,
Supplies carefully secreted and buried,
Providing sustenance for leaner times.

Brushing through the rustling bracken,
Wandering quietly, delightfully lost,
In this enchanted place it's easy to believe,
That faeries store their woodland gold.

**Fiona Hooper** © 2021

Autumn magic is alive in this forest.

On a patchwork of russet and gold.

Weaving warmth with the ambers and yellows

Tasteful tapestry, stunning and bold.

With comic suit, the evergreens ply us.

At the feet of ash grey, noble hosts;

who invite, looming brothers behind them…

Like pale shadows of slender cream ghosts.

Oh! That carpet of orange astounds me!

As does contrasts of powder blue skies.

All nature and forest in Autumn

plays music my soul amplifies.

**Roz Ottery** © 2021

## *Autumn's Glow*

**Oil on canvas, 60 x 60 cms**

As summer's emerald brilliance fades,
The changing season heralds autumn's glow,
Shimmering leaves respond to shorter days,
And create a spectacular fiery show.

A rich mosaic of golds, reds, and russets,
This feast for the eyes is a perfect delight,
Set against violet peaks and azure skies,
These vibrant colours set the scene alight.

The silver birches with their tapestry bark,
Papery layers with silvery edges curling,
Gently their leaves flutter to the forest floor,
Nutrients into the cycle of life returning.

The low sun now rakes across the valley,
Winter's icy fingers have marked their trails,
And brushed across the towering heights,
Adorning them with glittering snowy veils.

This land as yet unspoiled by the hand of man,
With majestic mountains, forests and lake,
Wild and untamed, with a primal beauty,
Let's keep it so, for nature's sake.

**Fiona Hooper** © 2021

In shimmering pastel autumn glows,

Bare aspen's argent barks Glint in paling auburn sun,

Dwarf trembling browning leafage,

Silent bar the thrum of lively pink bibbed Calliope,

hid in blazing gold leafed foliage,

Falling steep to lakes still slate,

Burning bright in high Montana's quiet sunset.

Beyond that grey lake's silent waters,

Deep within dark whistling forests,

Under purple powdered mountains,

Bloated grizzlies gorge on fresh pink salmon

And luscious red and purple huckleberries,

Preparing now for winter's lengthy hibernation.

Below, in sluggish rusting meadows,

Sensing subtle threat pervading,

Nervous mule deer sniff cool air,

And flee to brush,

Spooked by noisy nothing,

And high, against a minty sky,

Towed by well drilled echelon,

Snow geese on their maiden journey,

Race in space with piercing wind,

Blown from Russia's icy steppes,

Trumpet loudly fall's final flourish.

In that ripe Cheyanne autumn,

Trees again drip leafy blankets,

Once again the blood moon rises,

Slowly to the dimming sky

And black flecked silence,

Once again autumn's blazing orange patterns,

Fade in time to season's end

And coming winter's monochrome,

When winter's foul sulks

Replace fall's gentler temper,

Oppress with cold malignant darkness

That slowly fading gold leafed world,

Where famished bison scratch forlorn,

Remnants of a once great herd,

Trickle, like a scorched valley's grim river,

Down frosted slopes to warmer plains,

Affirm, for hunter and the hunted,

Fall's great exodus has begun.

And as the blood moon gently wanes,

From dreamy smoking tepees,

Mournful songs of Cheyanne ghosts,

Rise in wind to noble eagles,

Echo loud in cold blue space,

Like the last wolf's final howl,

Aching chants forever warning,

Our shrinking green and golden places

Live only as long as the last one to remember.

**Martin Goldie** © 2021

# Sheltered Valley

**Acrylic on canvas, 60 x 60 cms**


Walk with me in this tranquil sheltered valley,
Nestled in the lee of the towering massif,
Feel the grasses brush against your knee,
And sense change coming as autumn passes.

The golden meadow now crisp and dry,
Caressed by the breeze it ripples and flows,
Rugged lilac mountains reaching to the sky,
Dusted with the first of the winter snows.

The air has an edge, a new colder bite,
As it seeps down from the ice bound peaks,
Morning mists clear to crystal sharp light,
As balmy autumn beats a hasty retreat.

It's a refuge from the worst of the weather,
Protected by its guardians silent and strong,
Where animals shelter and gather together,
A haven where winter can be cruel and long.

Admire for now these richly glowing hues,
Before winter imposes its icy palette,
Warm golds replaced by greys and blues,
The valley clothed in its seasonal jacket.


**Fiona Hooper** © 2021

Ending our numb trudge below these slopes
We arrive as vacuums, stuffed with inertia,
Dragging our baggage of drains upon spineless hopes.
Stubborn. Completed. Set on empty stasis
Set to ignore the squirming of our parched organs,
Endure and relish the salivating,
The rumbling, the craving, the lapping towards -
-
A hollow hole again.
Rest, at last – A cell barred against pain.

Dreams have spiralled from memory,
Illusions merge with awakened observations
As we see – allow ourselves to see -
The odorous breeze that sweeps this porous scene,
The intangible murmurs wafting from pine to eye,
Weaving their thread through trees, souls and reeds.
Distant summits entice our feelings up,
Deep within the intestinal knots stirs an upward pulse,
A sudden thrust fettering our gaze to
An illusory peak.
Shards, rays, flurries
Of fogged glimpses provide the paint, the wind the soothing balm,
Caressing our senseless nerves to sculpt companions
Upon the solitude.
Rooted passive to the earth,
Our eyes regain this central perspective,
Primed again to channel an unknown, welcome vision.

We arrived as vacuums, stuffed with inertia,
Dragging our baggage of drains upon spineless hopes.
We leave as vessels, filled with forces
Lugging our cargo of hopes upon bolstered backs.

**Oscar Nicholson** © 2021

## Moored By The Mill

Oil on board, 10 x 12 ins

# Moored By The Mill

**Oil on board, 10 x 12 ins**

Drifting gently along the meandering river,
Its banks overgrown with shrubs and trees,
I find some moorings at the river's bend,
A place to shelter from the gusting breeze.

As I gaze across at the old white-topped mill,
I can imagine the creak of the wooden sails,
But the building is silent, abandoned now,
No more will it turn and tell us its tales.

The clouds have gathered, looming above,
Driven by the wind across this flat ground,
Yet still the sun breaks through their cover,
And boats and mill with light are crowned.

It's a peaceful spot, a tranquil place to rest,
Water gently lapping as it flows round the hull,
Dragonflies and birds accept our calm presence,
And the world is caught in a delicious lull.

A boat glides quietly past, using the river's flow,
But here we'll stay and experience the thrill,
Of an approaching dusk and a velvety night,
In this idyllic place, safely moored by the mill.

**Fiona Hooper** © 2021

Under winter sky the river flows by

Dark depths alight

In the random moments clouds gap.

Waves slap, slap.

Wind gusts, ruffling reeds and feathers

Blades of windmill captured

Set pivoting on axis, moaning

Cattle hidden, lowing

Sounds dance in symphony

A soothing mixed cacophony

A unique and captivating blend

corralled at river bend

Until the weather passes

I am a silent witness

Taking in my fill

Of an unexpected mooring by the mill.

**Skylar J Wynter** © 2021